The
Truth About
Embroidery Business
Success

7 Elements to a Highly
Profitable Home-Based
Embroidery Business

By

Joyce Jagger

The Embroidery Coach

Joyce Jagger
Binghamton, NY
www.TheEmbroideryCoach.com

Limits of Liability and Disclaimer of Warranty
The author and publisher shall not be liable for
your misuse of this material. This book is strictly
informational and educational purposes.

Warning – Disclaimer
The purpose of this book is to educate and entertain.
The author and/or publisher do not guarantee that anyone
following these techniques, suggestions, tips, ideas, or strategies
will become successful. The author and/or publisher shall
have neither liability or responsibility to anyone with respect
to any loss or damage caused, or alleged to be caused, directly
or indirectly by the information contained in this book.

ISBN 978-1477642108

Acknowledgements

My Husband: For all of the help that you give me and the love that you show me through out each day. I am so grateful that you have given me the freedom to spend many hours in this office as I am learning more about how to excel in this business. The more I learn, the more I can share with my students to make their lives easier. Without you I would not have had the time or the patience to write this book.

To My Children: I am so lucky to have 3 wonderful children that are constantly encouraging me. My son David runs the embroidery business that I started 34 years ago, my daughter Carolyn arranges all of my travel and my daughter Kathleen does all of my proofreading. You are all very successful adults in your own right! I am so proud of you!

Ernie Skaidas: My Accountant for all of your teachings about how I should run my embroidery business. Without your help and guidance I could not have created my very profitable embroidery business pricing structure. I have been able to teach this same concept to hundreds of embroiderers and it has surely made a difference.

Tracy Trill: Thank you for being my sounding board! It has been great having such a willing student to be able to bounce ideas off! Not only are you a great student, you have become a very trusted friend.

To my past embroidery business employees: Many of them were very instrumental in the growth of my embroidery business. Some of those same employees are still there working with David today. You were very instrumental in helping me create my training programs. You made it possible for me to perfect my techniques. Thank you very much!

To all of my embroidery students and consulting clients: You are why I do what I do day in and day out. I love what I do and to be able to share the knowledge with you that I have gained over the past 34 years is such a gratifying feeling. Thank you for all of the wonderful words of kindness and appreciation that I receive on a daily basis. I will strive to continue giving you my best and grow with you.

"Your On-Line Marketing Classes Have Saved Me A TON Of Time Setting Up My New Website"

I want to thank you for all the valuable information I have received on your embroiderytipsandmore.com website, as well as the webinars I attend every month. I had already been in the embroidery business for about 14 years when I discovered your training site. I was SURE that I knew it all, but figured I'd check it out. There are many shortcuts and more ways to do things than I had originally thought. I had only been digitizing basic designs for several years when I started to take your webinars. The lessons I received have added greatly to my knowledge of the Pulse DGML software. I have learned ways to work with alphabets and monograms that were never taught in any of the Pulse webinars that are so easy, I wonder why no one ever thought of them before!

Your on-line marketing classes have saved me a TON of time setting up my new website. My old site took months of work, and didn't look half as professional as the new one does with your training. I recommend your site to all the "Newbies" that I come across in the business. I'm sure I'll be taking your classes for a long time to come!

Brenda Adams
Artistic License
Weymouth, MA

"I Consider Myself Very Fortunate To Have The Opportunity To Learn From Her. She Is Amazing!"

I have been a member of Joyce's Embroidery Club for over 2 years. Through Joyce's private lessons, online videos, webinars and her blueprint for pricing embroidery, I have been able to gain confidence in running my own business. I know that I can always get a knowledgeable, complete and accurate answer to any of my embroidery questions from Joyce! Her knowledge and expertise is vast and she sincerely wants to see the embroiderers she works with succeed in their own businesses. *Joyce generously makes her experience in running a successful embroidery business available to us. Whether it be the mechanics of producing embroidery or the logistics of marketing and running an embroidery business, you can always count on her to have a solution for any challenging situation. I consider myself very fortunate to have the opportunity to learn from her. She is amazing!*

Suzee Bailey
Golden Crossings Embroidery
Colchester, CT

"She Truly Cares About Your Success"

Joyce Jagger's advice is an important asset to any embroidery business. Her vast familiarity with the genre and the business helped me become not just an embroidery machine operator, but an accomplished embroider and business owner. She has a tremendous amount of knowledge to share and truly cares about your success.

Bob Dandurand
Elite Skate and Embroidery
Warwick, RI

"We Never Thought That We Would Get As Far As We Have So Fast!"

I have to tell everyone that in the short three years that my husband and I have been in this crazy embroidery business, we never thought that we would get as far as we have so fast. Joyce's websites, webinars and personal guidance have been amazing! I can't say where we would be if it wasn't for her. Her vast outstanding knowledge of this business is just what every good embroider needs to become great!
Thank you so very much!

Amanda & Howard Potter
A&P MasterImages
Utica, NY

"Thank You For Making Things Much Easier For Everyone To Grasp How To Embroider Professionally!

I just wanted to send you a quick note on how much you have helped my embroidery business. When I started a few years ago I was looking for more training so I could get more fluent with my digitizing and hooping different items. I then found your site www.EmbroideryTipsand More.com and was very impressed with all the how to videos and to learn that I could attend different online seminars on top of it all was just the icing on the cake in my book. Some of the seminars I attended were on small lettering, working with stock designs, Monograms and many more. Your latest seminars on building a website have been fantastic. Even though I already have a website in place I learned so much from your seminars that I am now making even more changes to my site and my blog is a great asset to my online presence.

My business would not be a growing business if I hadn't stumbled on your training website so Thank You for making things much easier for everyone to grasp how to embroider professionally!

Tina Kleppe, Owner
Embroidery Gals.com
Dawson, ND

Contents

1

Planning Your Day – Setting Your Goals – Planning Your Business

*Create a Simple Working Plan that is a true
Road Map or Guide for YOU to follow*

23

#2

Create A Full Off Line And On Line Marketing System

*A Plan & Method Of Staying In Touch With Current Customers
A Plan To Create Many New Prospects and Customers.*

49

#3

Knowing How To Price Your Products Or Services For Profit

*Develop A Total Pricing Structure To Cover Every Pricing Scenario
In You Business*

89

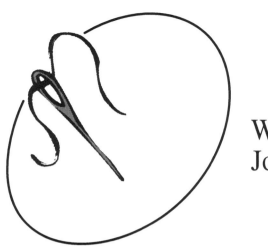

Who is
Joyce Jagger?

Joyce Jagger is The Embroidery Coach who simplifies the complex world of embroidery into easy to understand lessons. From learning how to hoop, to creating complex designs, to pricing your embroidery, to putting your business online, Joyce can help you move forward in your business.

She has spent her entire life sewing and creating many one of a kind gift items, home decorating projects and clothing for herself and her children.

She started her embroidery business in 1978 after her youngest daughter went off to college. The small home based business grew into a medium sized successful multi-head embroidery business.

In 2002 she started Designer Marketing Inc., her own training and consulting business helping new embroiderers get started and helping existing embroiderers increase their bottom line.

In 2006 she opened up an on-line Embroidery Video Training site, www.EmbroideryTipsAndMore.com. This embroidery training site is a membership site that teaches all phases of embroidery basics. There are over 175 videos on-line ranging from machine basics to how to hoop and embroider many types of garments. She even shows how to repair mistakes!

Her Embroidery Video Training website has changed and grown into TheEmbroideryTrainingResourceCenter.com. She has added more information and levels of membership along with sending out email weekly lessons. Once a month she holds an embroidery training webinar teaching many embroidery and business techniques. The techniques taught during these training sessions will work for any type of embroidery software or most sized embroidery businesses and are available for purchase after each webinar.

She has also created a new website, EmbroideryExpertsAcademy. com where she will help you on a personal level to excel in whatever area of your embroidery business that you feel you need. This can be either the applications, design or the business side of your business.

She teaches the Tajima by Pulse DG/ML software. Training is available on site at your location, in her office or on-line for all levels of the Tajima by Pulse software, and for all student skill levels.

She is currently on the Advisory Board of an embroidery trade magazine, "Stitches Magazine" and is a contributing expert to The Business Spotlight" in that magazine. She also writes articles that are featured in Ezine Articles on the internet.

This current book is the second edition of "The Truth About Embroidery Business Success". She also has several books and articles that are available for the Kindle through Amazon.com.

Joyce's passion is to help get the new embroiderer off to a fast start! She also loves to help the existing embroiderer improve their skills so that they can provide higher quality embroidery and increase their profitability!

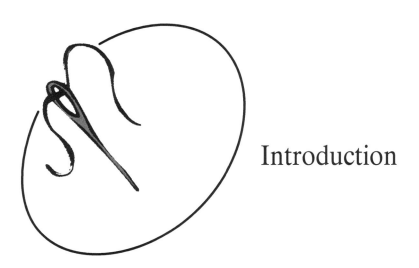

Introduction

The original "The Truth About Embroidery Business Success" was published in 2010. This is an expanded and updated version of the same book. The links in this book have been changed; there is an additional chapter that is very important in running and growing your embroidery business, and I have included additional content in each chapter.

I have worked with many students in the past few years helping them with many of the same issues that you may be experiencing. I want you to have the information that you need to start your embroidery business correctly and grow your business quickly! There is no need for you to wander through this business trying to find the right answers when they are readily available to you.

"Smart people learn by their mistakes, but
Smarter people learn by other peoples mistakes."
~Author Unknown~

That is an excellent quote that I received from my business coach, yes I still have a coach, and it really means a lot to me. There is so much truth to this quote and this is my goal for all of my students. You are all very smart people, but I want you to learn from my mistakes!

Starting a new business is not easy. It is very exciting, but it can be extremely overwhelming with all that you need to learn in a very short time. One of the big questions is, where can I go to get all of the knowledge that I need in order to get started so that I do not make costly mistakes? This is what I struggled with when I first got started. The information that I needed was not readily available like it is today. There is a lot of information available on the internet and through the embroidery machine manufacturers that was not there when I started my embroidery business.

"How Do I Run My Embroidery Business And Make A Profit?"

One of the big areas of training for new embroiderers that is not easily found, is the area: "How do I run my embroidery business and make a profit?" This was a huge struggle for me and this is a real battle for most embroiderers. It is not the kind of business that most people understand. When I started my business, I did not have an accountant. When I started working with an accountant, it was very hard for him to understand my type of business. Yes, like any other business, I needed to make a profit but there was a lot more to it than that.

I had to have my accountant come into my business and actually work with me and watch everything that was going on so that he could understand the problems and many issues that I was struggling with. The embroidery business seems to be unlike any other type of business! It is labor intensive, more so than many other types of businesses.

It was not until I almost lost my business and educated my accountant that he could actually help me turn my business around and make it profitable.

Before I begin sharing the knowledge that I have gained along the way, I want so tell you how I started my embroidery business. It was not the correct way to get started; I made so many mistakes.

Learn From My Mistakes

There is no reason why you should start your embroidery business without the sufficient knowledge that will help you succeed right from the very beginning.

This book will only touch the surface of what you should learn before you actually start your business, but it will help get you on the right track and get you thinking about what is actually involved and the correct steps to take.

There is a lot of information available today and it is always a good idea to absorb all of the knowledge that you can get before you get started. If you are someone that has already started your own embroidery business and are not having the type of success that you had envisioned, then this book will help you get on the right path to developing your own profitable embroidery business.

The Wrong Way To Started

I started my own embroidery business over 30 years ago as a result of a good friend asking me to embroider a name on a jacket.

That was the beginning of a very small embroidery business that started in my home, but grew and became a medium sized multi-head (37 heads) embroidery business.

I gave my gift items to many friends and family members for special occasions and this blossomed into a business that I loved and had a lot of fun with. Free word of mouth advertising helped my business to grow very rapidly and I had to move it from my home into a retail location. I soon found myself with so much work to do that I did not have enough time to get it all done, even after hiring some help.

I did no preparation or research and had no idea how to run a business. I loved what I was doing and it did not seem like work!

When I was asked to put that first name on a jacket, I knew almost nothing about embroidery except that it could be done on my regular home machine. The instruction manual that I received when I purchased my machine said that it could be done. This was back in 1978 when they did not have home embroidery machines. It was a regular home sewing machine that had a zigzag stitch. That home machine with a zigzag stitch opened up a whole new world for me.

I had no one that I could call on for any type of training or advice. I found myself running like a mad person trying to learn how to do the type of embroidery that my customers were asking for, and run a business at the same time. I look back and wonder how I ever made it!

Starting your new embroidery business without enough preparation and research is the perfect recipe for financial disaster! Starting your own embroidery business is just like starting any other type of business and should not be entered into without a lot of preparation just because you like to sew or do embroidery.

Embroidery is an exciting business and can be a very lucrative business when it is started properly with all of the right resources and preparation.

7 Key Elements To A Highly Profitable Home Based Embroidery Business

Only 79% of the embroiderers that start their own business survive past the first year! Many others fail within the next 2 or 3 years. This is a sad fact and it has little to do with the intentions and effort of the embroiderer. It has more to do with having the right systems, approach and tools in place.

There are 7 key elements that I have found to be very important during the early phase of starting your own embroidery business or trying to achieve a highly profitable embroidery business.

1. Planning

2. Marketing

3. Pricing

4. Niche Marketing

5. A System To Organize And Manage Your Business

6. Finding Good Employees

7. Education

8. Action Plan

The first 7 are the Key Elements; No. 8 is your Action Plan. It is very important to start taking action immediately. So many times we find a good book and discover that it has a lot of great points, but after we finish the book and lay it down, we do not go back and take the steps that have been suggested to take to make our situation better.

I want to help you understand the importance of these key elements and help you avoid the mistakes that I made when I started my embroidery business. Read all the way through this book first before you try to create your Action Plan. Go back and re-read each chapter again. As you are reading it for the second time, concentrate on each chapter and apply what you are learning as you create your Action Plan. This is very important. Each time I read something I learn from it. When I go back and read it again, I am amazed at what I missed!

If I had had a guide to get me started, I would have seen a return on my investment much sooner and it would have saved me many years of frustration and anxiety. I was determined to have the best quality embroidery in my area and give the best customer service that I could afford to give. Through much trial and error, I was able to accomplish this.

I want to help you in your journey to building your own embroidery business; the type of business that gives the satisfaction that every business owner searches for!

Joyce Jagger

The Embroidery Coach

Make sure to sign up for my FREE Ezine, **Embroidery Business Success Tips**, that I send out every other Thursday. http://www. theembroiderycoach.com/Newsletters/newsletter_signup.htm

Don't miss out on your chance to receive a lot of FREE valuable information with each issue.

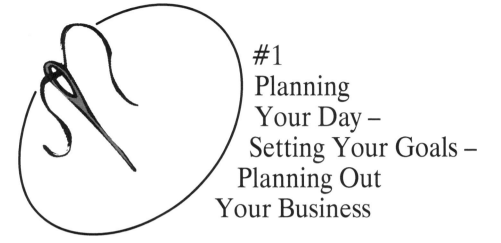

#1
Planning
Your Day –
Setting Your Goals –
Planning Out
Your Business

"The majority of men meet with failure because (they don't create) new plans to take the place of those that fail."

~Napoleon Hill~
Motivational Expert

Create a Simple Working Plan that is
a true Road Map or Guide for YOU to follow

You started your embroidery business because you had a dream about being your own boss and you wanted to create a product that you were really passionate about! Most embroiderers are really passionate about what they do but passion alone will not bring you business or money! You must have a plan; a plan that will be the roadmap to take you where you want to go.

If you have already started your business and have not created your business plan, then this is for you! If you have not yet started your embroidery business, this information will help to get you started in the correct way right from the beginning! If you created a plan a long time ago because you were told you had to have a business plan but stuck it in a drawer never to find it again, this is also for you!

Starting a business without a plan in place or a roadmap to follow is a tough way to get started. If you have no direction, you really do not know where you are going, how you are going to get there and have no idea where you are going to end up!

I actually created many short term plans in the early days of my embroidery business when I was growing quickly. With these short term plans, I knew what I had to do to achieve the goal that I was working towards, but I didn't realize that what I really needed was a real business plan.

Purpose Of The Business Plan

The main purpose of a business plan is to give you a clear direction and guidance on how you intend to run your embroidery business and plan for future growth. With this plan you will be able to analyze and measure each step along the way to ensure that you truly are on the right path.

Writing a business plan is not as tough as it seems; the hardest part is getting started and knowing where to start. I found that by taking it piece by piece; the job was much easier and I really could not believe what I learned as a result of taking the time to do it. To this day, I refer to my business plan each time I get a new idea to see if I am going to be able to easily work that into the plan. If not, then I will give my idea a lot of considerable time and thought before I actually go in and change my plan. Sometimes this works, sometimes it does not and I have to scrap the idea. Not every idea I get will work and if it does not help to increase my business or enhance my business in any way, then I have to forget about that idea.

With a written business plan, one that is actually usable, it helps to keep you on course so that you do not spend too much time on shiny objects that come across your path and distract you.

Many business plans look great on paper, but do not succeed in real life. Make sure that you are writing a plan that will work for you in the real world! The end result is very rewarding and a real eye opener.

Creating A Plan Starts One Day At A Time

Creating a Plan has to start with planning out each and every day. Without creating a plan to follow throughout your day; for your business and personal life, you have no idea where you are going to end up at the end of that day. I cannot emphasize that enough!

I found through experience that I was much happier when I had a truly effective blueprint for running my business and my personal life. Imagine how wonderful it would be to wake up in the morning and know that when you get into your office you are in total control and know exactly what you are going to be doing. Your business plan is on the corner of your desk in a binder and your to do list for today is sitting right in the center of your desk! This is the kind of organization in your life that you can have and it is not hard to create.

Creating a Simple Working Plan starts at the end of every day. This is the time that I create a list of everything that I have to do, set my priorities, and lay out my plan for the following day. When setting my priorities and creating my plan; I write down 3 major items that are a must to get done and I work around those 3 items. I have found that when I write down more than 3 major items and I cannot complete them, it creates feelings of frustration and failure. The secret is to keep it simple and this will work for you.

Creating my daily plan only takes a few minutes at the end of my work day and I am ready for the following day. I start out each morning knowing exactly what I have to do. This takes all of the anxiety and frustration out of where to begin. With my plan in front of me, I can quickly get started.

Once you are in the habit of creating a daily plan, now it is time to begin creating a weekly plan. Take time out at the end of the week to plan out your following week. By Friday afternoon, you already know how much work you have in house that needs to be scheduled for the following week. Yes there are jobs that arrive each and every day but if you take the time to plan your next weekly schedule on Friday afternoon, you will be able to see where you can slide in the extra jobs that come in during the following week.

After you have developed the habit of planning for a few weeks, and you know how much work you can accomplish in a week, you can then begin to really think about how to plan out your entire business. Does that mean that you plan your business around just exactly how much work you can accomplish in a week, absolutely not! This is just the beginning. It is like the beginning of an action plan to really start planning your business.

What if I am just starting my embroidery business and have no idea as to how much I can do in a week? Start timing all of your actions and tasks. A simple kitchen timer or an inexpensive stop watch will work beautifully for your timing.You need to figure out how much work you can do in a day and plan out from there. If you do not know what you are going to be able to do in a day, figure it out on an hourly basis and multiply from there. Do not forget to plan for break times, lunch time and interruptions to your day. All of these add into the amount of hours that fill up your day.

Begin With A Simple Plan To Check Your Progress

There are simple business plans and there are very complex or formal business plans. If you are not seeking any financial assistance, you will not need a complex or formal business plan. A Simple plan or Roadmap to check your progress and make sure that you are staying on track is all that is necessary. You want something that you are truly going to use and you do not need to spend weeks on this plan. Creating a simple plan should not take any more than one week. Many times it can be done in a weekend.

For a simple basic plan for internal use only, it is not necessary to spend countless hours researching and getting facts. However; it is to your benefit to know exactly what the competition is doing in your market and what you can do to make yourself standout from this competition. You also need to know exactly why you want this business and what goals you intend to reach as a result of this business.

It can be a simple 5-10 page plan that will work for most small to medium sized embroidery businesses, or as complex as you want it to be. This all depends on your situation. Make sure that you are creating a plan that is real!!

Progress To A Formal Business Plan

If you are going to seek financial assistance then you can expand on your simple business plan. You can do the research that is required to get the facts and figures to complete the formal business plan while you are using your simple business plan. You will be using this business plan, or roadmap, on a regular basis to check your progress.

With the proper projections written into your business plan, you can foresee trouble spots and pro-act, instead of react, to obstacles that may be put in your path. A Business Plan is not cut in stone and many times, I have found that I needed to take a totally different direction. This is very common and happens to most embroidery businesses.

If that happens to you, don't forget to go back to your plan and make the necessary adjustments and changes.

It is extremely important to have this guide or roadmap to keep you on that correct path. It is so easy to wander away from your main course and objective; but having a good plan to refer back to will help you stay on that main course and make the right decisions.

Easy Way To Get Started

The easiest way to get started is to start by gathering all of your information piece by piece and filing it into a three ring binder. Purchase a simple binder along with dividers for each of the 7 sections of your plan. Label all of the tabs on the dividers with the names of each element in the business plan. As you gathered the information file it into the divided section of the binder. The basic elements of the business plan are as follow:

- Executive Summary
- Business Description And Vision
- Definition Of The Market
- Marketing And Sales Strategy
- Organization And Management
- Financial Management
- Appendix

You do not have to work on each section until it is completed. You can work on several sections at once as you have the information. When you are working on your plan in pieces, it does not seem to be such a huge task.

(I have given you a fill in the blanks "Embroidery Business Plan Template". You can go to website http://www.embroiderybusinesssuccess.com/book-order-success/ and register to receive your copy of the template. Print out a copy of the template so that you can start working on your plan immediately.)

The business plan is divided into sections. As you fill out each page, you will file it into the applicable section of your binder for that page.

Even though the Executive Summary appears first, this is the last section that you will actually work on. This is the two page summary of your entire plan. We will discuss this at the end of this chapter.

Business Description And Vision
Mission Statement

Briefly state in one or two sentences the reason why you want to start your embroidery business or if you have an existing business, why you are in business and then you can follow this by creating your company goals. You need to have a "Big Why" in order to succeed in this business. You must know what that "Why" is and see if you have the determination to stick with it when things get tough and sometimes they really do! To start this process, grab a blank sheet of paper and think about what you really want to do. Answer each one of the following questions thoroughly and then condense them into a concise Mission Statement. This is letting everyone know why your company exists and how it is going to operate. You also want to explain why someone should do business with you.

- Why do you want to start an embroidery business? If you have already started your embroidery business, why did you start it?

- What is the primary purpose for this business?

- What type of core values will you be incorporating into your business?

Example: ABC Embroidery Company will offer the highest quality promotional products to the small business community so that they can increase their visibility in their marketplace.

Vision Statement

What is the vision that you have for this business in the future? This will be a statement about the growth and potential of the company.

- What does a successful embroidery business look to like to you?

- What do you see for this company 5 years into the future?
- How do you plan to accomplish the goals for the company 5 years into the future?

Example: ABC Embroidery Company will be the largest embroidery business in the Tri-Cities area by consistently providing the highest quality products and exceptional customer service to the Small Business Community.

Business Goals

Now it is time to write down your goals. I am sure that you have heard "Write Down Your Goals" many times. That was another area that I really struggled with. I had no idea how to write down goals to make them work. Oh Yeah! I want to be rich! I want to have a really great business! Those types of goals are not really tangible goals that you can shoot for. You need to have specifics such as "I want to acquire 10 new customers this month". This is something that you can truly work towards. With such a specific goal in mind, you can create a plan to actually reach that goal! Once you get the concept down, it will be easy to create your plans and work towards your goals.

- What is your main goal for the first year?
- What are your additional goals for the first year?
- What is your main goal for the second year?
- What are your additional goals for the second year?
- What would be your main goal 5 years into the future?

Major Business Objectives

In this section you should use bullet points to explain all of your plans. Include in this section if you have any intentions of filing for "Women Owned" or "Minority Owned" status for the purpose of procuring government contracts; however this is not a priority for a start up.

- What are your specific plans to start or expand your embroidery business?

- What are your specific plans to start or increase your production? Is this an expansion of an existing product or service?
- Will you be offering new products or services?
- Will you be adding any professional sales and marketing teams?
- Do you have plans to increase your staff?
- What contingency plans do you have in place in case there is a change in the economy or the industry? In today's economy, this is extremely important and one of the most important aspects of your business plan. You must be prepared for the inevitable.

Description and History of the Business

What is the physical address of the business? If it is a new startup, where will the business be located?

Existing Business

Give a total picture of the existing business. Make sure that you include answers to all of the following questions. Describe the business in chronological order (including dates) in this section. The would include the year the business started, when additional products were added, when additional equipment was purchased, when problems occurred and what you did to overcome them and grow.

- How long has the company been in business?
- What is the sales and profit history?
- How many employees
- What type of problems have you encountered in the past and what how did you overcome them?
- What successes have you had that has helped you to grow?
- Any previous owners?

Definition of the Market

Describe the Embroidery Industry Market as a whole and the Outlook for that market. The embroidery industry has changed during the past few years. In the past most of the embroidery was produced in large factories on large multi-head machines. The industry trend is moving towards most of the embroidery being done in small shops on single head and smaller muti-head machines. Many of these businesses are home based using one or two single head machines.

Identity your Target audience within that Market

- What are the specific needs in your Target Market?

- Provide a profile of your Target Market?

- What share of this Target market do you currently have or will acquire?

Description of Products/Services

Describe all of your products and services and explain how your products and services compare to the competition. What makes your products or service different or stand out from the competition.

Products

- List all of the products that you currently provide or intend to sell. This should include all of your embroidered products, such as shirts, caps, jackets, etc.

- What products do you have to offer that a competitor is not already offering?

Services

- List all of the services that you will provide.

Example: Embroidery

　　　　　　　Sewn Twill

　　　　　　　Alterations

- List any extra services that you offer such as FREE delivery within a certain area.

- Do you or do you plan to offer any special services.
- Do you plan to offer contract embroidery? (Embroidery on other peoples products that are sent to you from dealers)
- Do you offer a specific service, quality or higher customer service than the competition?

Machine/Equipment Required

List all of the equipment that will be required for your startup or expansion. Attach pictures or brochures of all of the equipment. State what equipment you plan to purchase. Be sure to include the brand name, description, equipment price and freight delivery price. Keep the types of equipment on separate lists.

Embroidery Equipment

- Will you need to purchase equipment?
- Do you need any embroidery design software?

Office Equipment

- Do you need any office equipment?
- Do you need any software?

Other Equipment – Do you need any other type of equipment?

- Pressing Equipment
- Steaming Equipment
- Sewing Equipment

Product Inventory Required

Will you need to purchase inventory? List the entire inventory that will be required along with the pricing of each item. It is also a benefit to include the selling price along with what your profit will be on an average. Obviously all jackets will not be the same price. Just use an average price for each item type.

Item Description	Your Cost including Freight	Selling Price	Profit
Jacket	$19.70	$39.95	$20.25

(For a formal business plan, you will also need to include the expected rates of inventory turnover, credit terms and delivery policies and your methods of inventory management, planning and control.)

Explanation of Inventory Turnover: The Inventory turnover is an equation that measures the number of times inventory is sold or used over in a period such as a year. The equation equals the cost of goods sold divided by the average inventory. The beginning inventory cost is added to the ending inventory cost and the total is divided by 2. This number is the average number used to figure your inventory turnover. Your Cost of Goods Sold is divided by the average number used to figure your inventory turnover. The final number is your inventory turnover rate.

The formula for average inventory:

$$\frac{\text{Beginning Inventory} + \text{Ending Inventory}}{2 \text{ (This is your average inventory number)}}$$

The formula for inventory turnover:

$$\text{Inventory Turnover} = \frac{\text{Cost of Goods Sold}}{\text{Average Inventory number}}$$

Assume cost of sales is $70,000 beginning inventory is $10,000 and ending inventory is $9,000. The inventory turnover equals 7.37 times ($70,000/$9500).

Credit Terms and Delivery Policies

State the credit terms, if any, that you have established with your customers. In the retail embroidery market, your customers should be paying a minimum of 50% down before you order their products with the balance being paid upon delivery or pickup. If you have online sales, they should all be prepaid. How long is the delivery time for each order?

Methods of Inventory Management

How will you manage your inventory? Are you keeping track of your inventory through your accounting program on the computer? Which program are you using?

Supplies Inventory Required

List all of the supplies including cost in each category separately.

- Embroidery Supplies

- Sewing Supplies

- Packaging Supplies

Customers, Contracts and Purchase Orders

- Do you have an existing customer base? List all of your existing customer accounts. (Include address) List the service or contract order customers separately from the retail customers.

- Do you have a list of prospective customers? (Include address)

- List all of your existing contracts and purchase orders that you have on hand. This is very important.

- If you are a startup, who will be your target market?

Suppliers

List the names and address of your suppliers, their buying terms and delivery policies. Do you take advantage of discounts offered by your suppliers?

- Blank Goods-T-shirts, caps, jackets, etc.

- Embroidery Supplies

- Office Supplies

- Packaging Supplies
- Freight Carriers such as UPS, Fed Ex, and USPS

Marketing And Sales Strategy

Target Market

Explain what specific type of group you will be marketing to. How large is your target market? Is this a local market or national market?

(You can find out a lot of this information in the public library. If you talk to the librarian, she will guide you to the correct information)

List the type of customers that you intend to market to and why you will be successful marketing to this customer group or niche. What is your experience with this market? (Do you belong to any of these groups? Do you have any type of associations with anyone in these groups?)

Example: Sports Booster Clubs

Fraternal Organizations

Corporations

- Have you done any research in this target market to see if what you have to offer will be in demand?
- Do you have more than one target market? This may be necessary if your target niche is a small one.

Existing Business

- Existing Customer Base – List the names and geographical location of each. (You have this on a previous page, but it must be repeated here.)
- Are they retail or wholesale customers?
- What is the percentage of sales brought in by each of your main customers?

- How will the new equipment affect your sales with your current customer base?

(A letter attached from your customers stating how their business will increase in the event you do acquire new equipment always looks good. This really worked for me when I needed a new 15 head embroidery machine. I got letters from all of my major dealers stating that they would send all of their cap business to me if I did get the machine. My banker was very impressed!)

- List Groups of customers that you intent to target – A fair amount of research is required for this category. You will need statistics or percentages of the market share that you expect to acquire and what type of an impact these targeted groups will have on your business.

(You can find out a lot of this information in the public library. If you talk to the librarian, she will guide you to the correct information)

Budget For Promotion

State what the total dollar amount will be of your budget for the first year. This must cover artwork, printing of brochures, letterhead, business cards, envelopes, tradeshows, website creation, automatic emailing system and packaging.

Go though the following questions and then create a listing for each of the different types of promotions that you have planned along with the cost of each. After you are finished you will have the total dollar amount for your budget for the first year.

- How will you advertise? – Current media selection and schedules (Small area tradeshows, radio or TV, ads in local papers)
- What will be the cost of this advertising?
- Every business today needs a website to market on line along with a total marketing system.
- Will you be creating this website or outsourcing it?

- What will be the cost associated with creating your on-line presence?

Personal Selling Efforts

What are your plans for getting the word out about your products and services?

- Do you have plans for doing any personal selling?
- Do you belong to any networking groups?
- Do you belong to any organizations?

Sales Training programs

- Will you be hiring salespeople?
- How will you train these sales people?

(You must have written plans & procedures in place so that each person is trained in the same manner. Training sales people is not an easy job; they usually have a tendency to do it their way and do not want to listen to you. Insist that they do or you do not have the right person.)

- What will you provide for them in the area of sales tools?

(Each sales person will need a complete set of embroidered samples along with brochures, pricelists, and order forms. They must have a way to give the customer a price on the spot in order to secure as many orders as possible quickly. Customers will lose confidence in your business if this is not done.)

Distribution Methods and Channels

- How are you going to sell your products? Retail store, sales people, website or all 3?
- If you are going to be doing business on-line, and you should, you will need a website.

(Regardless of what type of embroidery business you have today, you need to add a website. Many customers today want to be able to go to the website and select their products rather than going into your retail store. Others want to see what type of selection you have and then go into your retail store to meet with you on a personal level. Customers today do not take you serious unless you have website.)

Sales Forecast/Projections

A Sales Forecast or Projections is necessary for a new or an existing business. You will start with a list of all of your expenses that you are incurring or expecting to incur on a monthly basis and then you will add sales to cover these expenses. When you are first starting you may have more expenses than sales. This is very common until you start receiving the orders. For an existing business you must start with your current sales and the past history of sales.

Provide a Sales Forecast for the next 12 months on a month by month basis. You will want to create a few different scenarios in your planning so that you can come up with an average sales figure. By that I mean, create some with selling your products and services together and create some just selling your services. If you are an embroidery business owner that will allow a customer to come into your shop with their own garment for you to add embroidery, that is one scenario. You will charge this customer a higher price for the embroidery alone, than you will a customer that purchases a garment and the embroidery together. You expect to make a profit on the garment as well as the embroidery. This way you will have a more realistic sales figure to use to create your Sales Forecast.

In creating these scenarios, you will need to figure out exactly what kind of a markup you are going to have for your products and services. If you do not know how to figure your embroidery pricing or product markup, I have a program that will be very helpful to you. You can find it at http://www.HowToPriceEmbroidery.com. This program will teach you exactly how to figure all of you expenses and create your price own lists. It will also create a quick price list for you after you add your figures.

Create 2 categories for your Sales. The shirts, caps, and etc will go into a Products or Resale category, your embroidery will go into your Embroidery or Services category. If you provide other services, such as alterations, add them as a subcategory under the Services category. Do not try to lump them together. This will not provide a true forecast. You want to plan for a slight increase in sales each month. This will show a steady growth for your business. You do not want to provide any unbelievable figures here. It would only create a problem for you later.

It is best to project 2 different forecasts. One will be for the best case scenario and the second one will be for the worst case scenario. If you are creating a formal plan for the purpose of seeking financing, the bankers want to see that you have contingency plans and will have the proceeds to repay your loan.

You must be very realistic in creating your Sales forecast. If you are adding more sales than expenses just to make it look good, it would only make you look like you do not understand or know the true purpose of this plan. The whole purpose of this exercise is to show what you are expecting for sales and growth and to see that you do understand a Sales Forecast. This is basically a Goal Sheet that you can use to work towards.

This may be an area that you will need help with. When I first started creating my Projections and Sales Forecasts, I worked with my accountant.

(I have created a program that will walk you through how to write your business plan and I teach you how to create your Sales Forecast/ Projections in that course. http://www.EmbroideryBusinessPlan.com)

Competition

It is very important to know your competition and know what they have to offer. It is not always easy to get their information. Check to see if they have a website. Have family and friends visit them to get all of the information that they can. This will help you to formulate your plan to offer something different or better.

- List the companies with addresses that compete with you.
- What the products and services do they offer?
- Do they have any type of service or product that makes them stand out?
- Do you have a way to position your product or service in your market place that is different than the competition?

Pricing Structure

This is very important. You must show exactly how you have created your pricing structure and what type of a markup that you have created.

- What are your pricing polices?
- What is your markup on your products?
- Do you have a markup on your service or do you use the markup on your products to create the profit for your business?
- Do you charge the customer that brings in their product for your embroidery more than you do the customer that purchases your product and service together?
- Do you have more than one price level?
- Do you have discount policies?

(I have created a program that will walk you through how to create your pricing structure http://www.HowToPriceEmbroidery.com)

Accounts Receivables – Credit Policies

New Businesses should always require a minimum of 50% down and the remainder on delivery in order to avoid accounts receivables. Retail sales businesses should never have accounts receivables.

For Existing Business with Dealer or Wholesale Sales:

- What are your payment and customer credit policies?

- Do you manage your receivables in such a manner that you are receiving payment on time?

- Do you offer a discount if they pay within 10 days? This is usually a good way to encourage the dealers to pay within that period, but you must figure this extra cost in when you are creating your pricing structure.

Organizational Plan
Legal Form of Ownership

What is the legal form of ownership of your business? Sole Proprietor, Partnership, Corporation or a Limited Liability Corporation? If you are expanding, this may be the time that you change your form of ownership such as going from a Sole Proprietor to some form of Corporation. You should discuss with your accountant the best option for you. Each business is different.

Business Ownership

- Names and Address of all business owners.

- What is the percentage of ownership for each person?

- Attach Personal Financial Statements for each business owner

(Attach a résumé or bio of each person involved in the business)

Management Organizational Chart

If you have any management employees, you must create a chart showing each one. If you do not have any at the present time but are planning on hiring management, then you will include them in this section. You must state what you are paying them at the present time and project how much you will be increasing their salaries and or benefits.

(Attach a short bio and résumé of each management employee)

- List names, position and compensation for each employee. Present and for the next 3 years
- Benefits for each

Outside Resources

List the name of each of your outside resources and state how you will benefit from each one of these resources.

- Attorney
- Accountant
- Insurance Agents
- Consultants
- Mentors

Personnel

New Business

If you have any employees, you must create a chart showing each one. If you do not have any at the present time but are planning on hiring employees, then you will include them in this section. You must state what you are paying them at the present time and project how much you will be increasing their salaries and or benefits.

- Will you need to hire employees right away or will you start out running the entire operation by yourself?
- Do you have someone in mind that you can call on to help out in case of an emergency or to do some off jobs?
- If you are going to hire employees, how will you train them?

Existing Business

- How many employees do you have at present?
- How many you project to hire within the next three years? Bankers, the SBA and Economic Development organizations

like to see that you are going to be adding several job positions if you are going to obtain financing. Sometimes a minimum is attached to a loan, depending on the avenue you are seeking to obtain the loan.

- What type of systems or training do you have in place for your current personnel and your future personnel?
- What type of training programs do you plan to implement?

Legal Form of Business

Attach your documents stating what type of business you are. Sole Proprietor, Partnership, Corporation or a Limited Liability Corporation.

Financial Plan

Include current Financial Statements of the Business – It is recommended that you have your accountant help you with all of these statements. They must be accurate and believable.

- Income Statement
- Balance Sheet
- Cash Flow projection for 12 months month-by-month. If this is an existing business, use the past historical information along with your projections that you created with your increased production.
- Breakeven Analysis – This will determine how many sales are required to recoup all of your costs.
- Projected Balance Sheet for 1 year, 2 years and 3 years.
- Personal Tax Returns or Corporate Tax Returns (if this is a corporation) for 3 years

If you plan on obtaining any type of financing through investors, then you may be required to furnish additional information.

Executive Summary

Even though you are working on this part last, this is the first section of your business plan. It is much easier to write the summary after you have everything else in your plan finished. This is a simple two page document that explains the basics of the business. You can use bullet points for most of this area. Keep it as brief as possible. This is extremely important.

Bankers will go through the summary first and if they are unhappy with it, they will not go any further. Your business plan will be rejected immediately. If they go through the Executive Summary and are happy with it and the organization of it; this may sway their decision quickly in your favor. This was my experience. Use bullet points to explain:

- Who you are
- Who owns the business
- What your products are,
- Who are your customers,
- The future plans for both you and the business.

When applying for a loan explain exactly how much money you are requesting, what you will use it for and how it will be repaid with company profits.

If you are looking for an investment partner, in addition to the above, explain what the partner's role will be in the business, the percentage of ownership and the estimated return on investment.

Keep it simple, easy to read, concise, well written and complete. Avoid any contractions or slang words. Keep your sentences short.

Putting It All Together

After you have finished your Executive Summary, you will place it as the first section of your plan. Create a Table of Contents ending with the Appendix and list each section along with the page numbers. Attach copies of all of your legal documents in this Appendix section. This may sound very elementary, but it is very important.

I have found that the bankers and investors would rather see your finished business plan in a 3 ring binder rather than a spiral bound report folder. This gives them the opportunity to remove the pages if they need to for an easy review process. Use a binder that has the see through opening in the front. Create a front cover that has your name, business name and address, your logo and the words Business Plan printed on it.

Every 30 days take out your plan and go over it to make sure that you are still on track. The perfect time to review your plan is after you have finished your monthly accounting. You can make adjustments and see exactly what progress you have made. You can compare your actual sales and profit to your Sales Forecast and see how close you are to staying on your target.

I know that this is a lot of work, but after you are finished you are going to feel like a load has been lifted off of our shoulders. It gives you such a feeling of accomplishment!

Creating a business plan or a road map must be a priority! Once done, running your business will be easier and you will have the tools to make better decisions for your business!

Getting Help With Your Embroidery Business Plan

I created a program at www.EmbroideryBusinessPlan.com to help walk you through your Embroidery Business Plan step by step. It is a program that will make creating your Embroidery Business Plan very simple. I show you how to create your Marketing Plan for an entire year and I also teach you during this process how to plan out every department within your business. This is very important in order to have a business that will run efficiently! This is just as important to the small one person embroidery shop as it is to the large multi-head embroidery shop.

***"The Embroidery Business Plan Course Really Helped Tie
All The Loose Ends Together!"***

I would like to thank you for all the great information you provide about running an embroidery business. It has been VERY helpful, particularly since I have decided to turn my operation into a full time business.

I have just purchased your Business Plan development course
as I am getting ready to go to the bank for funding to expand the
business. I have a business plan that is about complete, but I felt that
it would be beneficial to get the input from your course, particularly
on the financial projections. I do have spreadsheets from our local
community college designed just for business plans to calculate all
of the financial information, however, they are very generic. After
reviewing Module 3, and the information you provided, I have to tell
you that I am really excited now to wrap it up and get to the bank.
It really helped tie all the loose ends together. THANK YOU!!!
Cindy Proctor
Busy Bee Embroidery
Dauphin, PA

Make sure that you get started immediately creating your own embroidery business plan, one that you can use on a daily basis and will give you that true roadmap to follow to your own embroidery business success!

#2
Create A
Full Off Line
And On Line
Marketing System

"Business is not just doing deals; business is having great products, doing great engineering, and providing tremendous service to customers.
Finally, business is a cobweb of human relationships."
~H. Ross Perot~

A Plan To Build Relationships With Current Customers
A Plan To Create New Prospects And Customers

When I first started my embroidery business I thought that all I had to do was put out my sign to let everyone know that I was now in business! I also placed a couple of ads in the newspaper. I thought that I would have all of the customers that I ever wanted or needed! It didn't quite work out that way!

I soon found out that getting customers was not as easy as I had envisioned! It really took a lot of work to get that steady flow of customers coming in the doors! I really loved what I did, but I had no plan in place to attract customers. Without a steady flow of customers, there is no business! This is not the right way to get your business started! I learned very quickly that I needed to have a plan in place for every aspect of my business, including marketing.

Marketing was a scary term when I first started my embroidery business. I was extremely timid and I discovered that most new embroiderers feel the same way. I was afraid to tell people what I was doing. After all, it was a "sewing business." I felt that no one would see me as a serious business owner, so I did what was natural. I stayed in my place of business, did my work and hoped that the customers would come to me. After all, I had my sign out and I had advertised in the newspaper. At a high cost I might add!

Getting Your Product Into The Hands Of The Right People

In looking up the actual meaning of the word Marketing, I found many. I have paraphrased very simply, the ones that mean the most to me.

- All of the things that you do to get your product in the hands of the Right People .

- The process that you go through to find the Right People to persuade to purchase your product or service. The operative word here is RIGHT as in Right People! The right people are the ones that need or want to buy your products or service.

So, Who are the Right People and How do we find the Right People? Every person is unique with his or her own ideas and belief system. Each person has their own perception as to what is right for them. We are looking for people that will fit within the framework of what we have to offer. Sometimes we have to expand our product line or services offered to attract more of those Right People!

People don't want to just buy your product; they are looking for the result of what your product is going to do for them. In Marketing Embroidery, it is all about the customer and what they want. It is not about you or your product!

"How do I know exactly what the customer wants and how I should market to them?" ASK them! The more you interact with your customers and show them that you have their interest at heart, the more they will know, like and trust you!

How long has it been since you actually communicated with your customers and asked them what you could do for them? This is not something that we normally think about or plan within our schedule, but it is a very effective way to find out what it is that your customer really wants. Truly listen to your customers when they are talking. There is a quote that I heard a long time ago:

"You cannot truly listen to anyone and do anything else at the same time."
~M. Scott Peck ~

I have found this to be true. You must pay close attention to your customer as they are talking to you. They will notice this immediately and appreciate your undivided attention! While I was preparing to write this book, I sent out a questionnaire to my students asking them one question. "What's your single most important question about Marketing Your Embroidery Business?" I received back over 100 responses. Many had questions that were related to cost and where their advertising dollars should be spent, but the majority wanted to know how to Market their particular embroidery business and attract new customers.

The Simplicity Of Creating Your Own Marketing Plan

"Failing to plan is planning to fail!"
~Author Unknown~

The most important process in getting ready to market your embroidery business is to create a working plan. You must have a Marketing Plan. This will help to keep you on the right track. If one strategy is not working you can go back and review your plan and make some changes, but without a plan you are just running in circles and do not have any idea as to what to do or where to go to get started.

Creating a working **Marketing Plan** sounds so scary, but it does not have to be that way. Sit down and write out a list of all of the things that you need to do to get started marketing to your customers. That is the beginning of your plan. Sounds simple doesn't it? Well it really is!

In this economy today we have to be very proactive and not sit and wait for the next customer to walk in the door. It is not going to happen. There are too many choices for them and we have to make sure that we are in their mind first and foremost so that they will think of us instead of the competition when they need our services. Without an actual working Plan it is very hard to be proactive.

I have heard from so many embroiderers that their business has dropped off dramatically due to the slower economy. This is such a scary feeling, but there are ways to prevent this and we will be talking about some of those ways.

The embroidery business world is usually slow at the beginning of the year and this is the time that you should be finishing up your year end book keeping and creating your new Marketing Plan for the coming year. This does not have to be a negative time. You need some time to clear your head from the busy holiday season and focus on creating a new plan and put it into action.

How To Start Creating Your Marketing Plan

Go through your sales records and determine which months are your busiest, then plan special promotions for your slower times. These slow periods usually happen about the same time every year, give or take a few weeks. You must have promotions planned ahead of time and ready to kick in just before the end of busy periods. It is easier to keep a steady flow going this way. Each year has its own challenges, but if you are proactive in your promotions, you will be more successful and will have less peaks and valleys.

Slow periods are also good times to develop new sales materials and samples. I used this time to develop new sales samples for my dealers and my retail store. I embroidered new designs on white felt and glued them into 3 ring binders to distribute to my dealer customers and I also created embroidered coasters out of felt to give away as samples. This is an excellent way to showcase your embroidery and a great leave behind when you are visiting a customer.

I created new samples for my showroom that were tagged with all of the information needed to help sell the item with as little of my time involved as possible in the sale. You need to block out some spare time in your working Marketing Plan to accomplish these little profitable, sales creating tasks.

What are all of the different seasons and holidays that we have? In the US we have Valentine Day, St. Patrick's Day, Easter, Mothers Day, Fathers Day, Christmas, Back to School, all types of sports including golf tournaments and everyone that you know has lots of special occasions. What are some of the items that you can offer for each one of these special occasions? What would you have to do to put together a simple plan to promote each one of these holidays and special occasions?

People need you and what you have to offer. All you have to do is make them aware of what you have, work with them to find out exactly what they are looking for and you can create the perfect relationship. I know it sounds so simple, but it really is!

Once I put a Marketing Plan together and started working my plan, I found out that letting everyone know that I was in business was not as hard as I thought that it was going to be. Did customers just flood through the door, No! I was constantly working my plan to gain new customers and keep the old ones happy.

> *"Most businesspeople are too busy working for their business or in their business and never find time to work on their business!"*
>
> ~Author Unknown~

Most Effective Ways To Market Your Embroidery Business

There are many ways to market your embroidery business but first I want to start out by giving you a few pointers about increasing your sales to your current customers, and then I will talk about prospecting for new customers. If is much easier and more cost effective to market to your current customers than constantly trying to find new ones!

Increasing customer sales with your current customer base is all about creating relationships. Creating good customer relationships is the most important duty that you have as a business owner and this is something that does not cost a lot of money. Many times it is the little unexpected things that we do that mean the most and keeps that customers coming back to our business over and over!

I purchased a program a from a large company and was shocked when I received a handwritten Thank you note in the mail. I have to tell you, I was extremely impressed at this gesture! Just a simple thank you card that only took the salesperson a couple of minutes to write meant a lot to me and I will remember that the next time that I decide to order another program.

Here are some simple ways for you to increase your customer sales.

- Offer Exceptional Customer Service
- More Low Cost – High Profit Services To Your Existing Customers
- Build A Relationship With Existing And Former Customers
- Plan A Customer Appreciation Night
- Create A Web Presence
- Offer More Than One Price Level Of Products

There are several Low Cost Methods of prospecting for new customers.

- Networking Off Line And On Line
- Donate Products & Services To Charity For Fund Raising Events
- Ask For Referrals
- Attend Trade Shows In Your Niche
- Offer To Trade Your Products & Services
- Press Releases

I will go over each of the simple ways to increase your customer sales and explain how to prospect for new customers. They can be done at the same time and many of them can be done on a daily basis as you are working within your business.

> *"Concentrate your strengths against your competitor's relative weaknesses."*
> ~Bruce Henderson~

Make Your Business Stand Out From The Crowd

Is there a service or a process that you can offer your customers that they cannot get from any of your competition? What is it that you can do to be more efficient than the competition? It is usually better to focus on being different in a particular market rather than trying to compete directly. Find a unique strategy or a way to position your products or your business differently in your current market place.

Spend some time educating your customers about the benefits, services and value that they will be receiving by doing business with you. Point out to them what you are doing that the competition is not doing. You do not have to say that the competition is not doing such and such; you just have to point out what you are doing that makes you different or better!

You cannot compete with the big manufacturers or embroiderers that have many multi-head machines when you are only a small shop with one or two heads. Don't even try. You must focus on what you do best in your smaller market. If you focus on improving one step or one process that can make you more efficient then this alone will help to make you more profitable!

Those large shops normally are not offering the type of customer service that you can offer. This can set you far above the larger shops and help to increase your customer sales. I have seen this many times. Many of the larger shops have systems all set that they will not steer away from, and they are usually profit focused instead of customer focused.

In order to be successful in this business, you must be customer focused. The profits will follow if that is the case! By finding your own unique way to stand out in the crowd, you will increase your customer sales naturally.

Offering Exceptional Customer Service to all of your embroidery customers will make you stand out and is extremely important in this competitive market place today!

7 Tips On How To Create Exceptional Customer Service

Here are 7 Tips that if followed by your entire organization, will change your business and give it a whole new life!

1. Start Out Each Day With A Positive Attitude!

2. Always Wear A Smile!

3. Have A Clean And Well Organized Environment!

4. You Must Be Willing To Work With Your Customer – Give Them A Reason Why They Need To Come Back!

5. Always Return Phone Calls And Always Respond To Emails!

6. Take Accurate Notes!

7. Never Show Anger With A Customer!

Start Out Each Day With A Positive Attitude!

There is no better way to create an atmosphere of Exceptional Customer Service than to be very upbeat and positive. When you have a great attitude it is reflected in everything that you do from waiting on a customer or getting employees started in the morning to finishing up the day with your family. Everyone around you benefits from your attitude. If you go into the office with a less than great attitude the entire organization is affected as well as your sales. No matter what your circumstances are, make sure that you reflect a great attitude in everything that you do! I remember from my Dale Carnegie training many years ago, "If you act enthusiastic, you will be enthusiastic!"

Always Wear A Smile!

Treating your customers with dignity and respect and always wearing a smile is the most important principal in creating exceptional customer service. This policy applies to direct contact in person as well as on the phone. People can tell how you feel and know if you are wearing a smile.

All of your customers should be treated as if they are the most important customer you have; it does not matter if they are a large account or a small one. Small accounts very often grow into large accounts.

You want your customers to feel that you are a partner in their business success; as a result you will receive more orders from these same customers. Excellent customer service goes a long way!

Have A Clean And Well Organized Environment!

Invite your clients or customers into a clean, well organized environment when they visit your showroom or office. This makes an important first impression.

Have your samples clean, well organized, in top quality condition and available for quick viewing as you are giving your presentation. Having a system in place makes your presentations easier and creates a feeling of trust with your customer.

If you have employees, have them wear shirts with your logo on them. This helps to create a feeling of unity and promotes team work and belonging! It is also another way to get your name out into the community as your employees go around town on their way to or home from work, wearing their shirts.

You Must Be Willing To Work With Your Customer – Give Them A Reason Why They Need To Come Back!

In the marketplace today, you need to be available and be willing to work with your customers in whatever capacity they are requesting. Today, the customers are demanding more and more from their suppliers in the way of services. If you do not meet their demands or wishes, someone else will. If you cannot meet their needs, given your situation, you must let them know up front.

Sometimes their requests seem to be unreasonable, especially delivery dates, but you must deliver on time or ahead of schedule in order to keep them happy and coming back for more. Customers become very unhappy and untrusting when they have to wait past the due date for goods they were promised.

Always Return Phone Calls And Always Respond To Emails!

When a customer or potential customer calls and has to leave a message, make sure that you get back to them in a timely manner. If you do not return their phone call they will feel that you do not want their business. All customers and potential customers need to be made to feel important!

This same principle goes for emails. If a person takes his time to email you, you must be courteous enough to take your time and reply to that email. They do not care how busy you are, their time is what is valuable to them, not yours! This type of excellent customer service is expected!

Take Accurate Notes!

Take accurate notes when you are working with a customer in person, over the phone or my email. They very often want to make a change in their order and this must be taken care of immediately as to not hold up their order.

You should have a system in place for this type of procedure with forms to use to take the notes or make changes. Make sure that the notes get connected to the customer's order. This is also true with email. If the customer sends you an email letting you know that he is requesting some changes in his order print it out and attach it to the original order. Then, bring it to someone's attention so that it is not missed.

If a proper procedure is not followed, the change can be missed and not carried through to the production process. This can be a potential disaster. If this occurs, you can lose a very valuable customer and many potential customers. Word travels very quickly and customers seem to spread the word faster if they are not happy than they do when they are happy.

Never Show Anger Towards A Customer!

If a problem or mistake has occurred by either you or the customer, never show anger towards that customer even if they show anger towards you. It does not matter if they are right or wrong; you must hold your head up high, keep your composure, and talk to them in a manner that will diffuse their anger.

Being angry does no one justice and in business it is one of the best ways to create bad relations. I have found many times by offering the customer a bit more or giving the customer a slight discount that they were much happier and I was able to smooth over a bad situation and build a better relationship with the customer at the end of the problem. They must be treated with dignity at all times.

Creating exceptional customer service is not hard! If you give all of your customers more than they expect, you will be greatly rewarded.

Offer Your Current Customers More Low Cost–High Profit Services

Offering other complimentary services is another way of increasing sales to your current customer base. Many of these additional services can be another low cost – high profit income center for you at a minimal charge to the customer. Your customers will respond positively to these added services. They would much rather keep their business in one location rather than have to shop around for the same services that you can provide.

- Bagging or Packaging Garments
- Sewing Services
- Banners
- Heat Press Transfers
- Promotional Products

Bagging or Packaging Garments

Offering to package the garments for a small price, such as .30 to .35 cents per each is a low cost – high profit service and is welcomed many times by clients. Plastic bags can be purchased for pennies and packaging garments is very inexpensive. This will help make your customers distribution easier and faster.

Sewing Services

- Sewing on labels (Private Labeling)
- Making repairs to damaged garments. This is far more cost effective than shipping back to the supplier and it saves production and delivery time.

- Adding a pocket to a shirt style that does not come with a pocket.
- Sewing on buttons
- Sewing on patches
- Hemming pants for work uniforms

All of the above sewing services are extremely low cost – high profit to you and can be billed out at a low price to the customer. The cost of equipment for these services is minimal. All that you would need is a serger and a straight needle sewing machine. Both machines could even be home sewing machines. They do not have to be commercial machines, although the commercial machines will run faster and outperform the home sewing machines. If you are adding this as a full time service you would definitely want to purchase the commercial machines. Your return on investment will be seen very quickly.

Many times you can pick up a used machine for a reasonable price. Whatever is available to and within your budget is the best way to get started. If you do not know what to charge for these services in your area, contact your local dry cleaners or tailors and ask what they charge. The pricing is not the same in all areas of the country. But you must keep in mind, you have to make money on this service or at least break even; so make sure that you are charging enough for this added service. This is another service of convenience to your customer.

These extra services can be added as a lead generator and as long as you break even on them but are making money on all of your other services, this will work out very effectively.

Banners and Table Covers

Custom designed embroidered and appliquéd banners and table covers are another low cost product and service that you can offer to your existing customers. By low cost, I mean low cost to you, not the customer. This is a low cost – high profit service that is not always available in every area and is needed by anyone that exhibits at trade shows, in parades or has any type of award ceremonies. Banners are not hard to make and the profit on banners is excellent. Networking through the organizations is the best way to acquire banner orders. The only equipment that is needed is your sewing machine, embroidery machine and a table. This is the equipment that you already use on a daily basis. This was always a very high profit income center for me.

Heat Press Transfers & Digital Printing

You can add a Heat Press and offer transfers or Digital Printing to be applied to lower priced garments. This is a great low cost – high profit addition to the embroidery business. This will help to keep more revenue in your shop. Customers love to be able to do one stop shopping and if you help them to plan their business promotional purchases, this is even better. Many times they do not want to spend much money on a garment if it is going to be used as a give-away to promote an event. Instead of having that customer go to a screen printer, and taking the chance of losing them, keep them right in your shop and offer the same type of service. You can accommodate small orders as well as large ones.

Transfers can be purchased very inexpensively and usually there is no set up charge. There are a variety of different types of transfers. For the low cost market such as Little League Sports teams you have numbers to be added to their uniforms or simple transfers to the front or back of T-shirts. This can also be done in vinyl lettering.

You can purchase a small or large quantity for your customer and just apply them as needed. Customers love a service like this and screen printers cannot work with small orders. Make sure that you charge your customer the purchase price of the transfers at the time that you purchase them and you can then charge a fee to apply each one as he orders the garments.

For the medium range market or the girls' sports teams such as Cheerleading and Dancing, you can add Rhinestone transfers. These are getting more popular all the time. Many times the transfers are perceived to be of higher value than the embroidery and you can charge more. You can even add stones in various places to enhance your embroidery.

There is a higher cost to get into the Digital Printing than just the Transfers but for some markets it is very lucrative and can be sold in the place of screen printing. Some smaller businesses find this to be a perfect solution to be able to cover all priced markets and create a very loyal customer following.

Promotional Products

Offering Promotional Products such as pens, pencils, key chains, mugs, trophies, buttons and many other items is another service that can bring in additional sales without you having to do much work. This is another low cost – high profit area of marketing. Your only involvement is showing the products, taking the order, placing the order with your supplier and delivering the goods when they arrive.

This is a service that most embroiderers are failing to offer their current customers. If you are not offering promotional products you are leaving a lot of money on the table that could be in your pocket. The sale of promotional products could be an add-on to all of your customer's regular shirt, cap or jacket orders. This is an inexpensive way for them to promote their business and you need to educate them of this fact. This is not something that most Small Business Owners may think of on their own without being prompted.

The use of promotional products is also an excellent way of promoting yourself. This would give you the ability to purchase your own promotional products at cost and it is much more effective and lower cost than any type of print media that you could use to advertise with.

When you can create a one-stop shop for your customers with many products and services, they are inclined to be more loyal and think of you first with all of their promotional and gift giving needs!

"Man's inability to communicate is a
result of his failure to listen effectively."
~Carl Rogers~

Connect With Your Customers To Build Good Customer Relationships

The best way to start building good customer relationships is to connect with each one of your current and lost customers. Start out by making 3 lists.

- Current High Volume Customers

- Current Lower Volume But Repeat Customers

- Former or Lost Customers

Create some scripts that will make it easier for you to talk to people. I have found that by having the scripts in front of me, it just made it easier as you are talking to them and you do not forget anything. You can also print out a script for each customer and fill in the blank as you are talking to them. Keeping notes makes it a lot easier to recall what they said for futures reference.

By taking the time to call these customers individually, you are showing them that you are sincere and that you really do care. Most of them will open up to you and be happy to talk to you and give you whatever feedback you are looking for.

(I have some sample scripts that you can print out and use on my website. http://www. EmbroideryBusinessSuccess.com/scripts)

Call each one of your customers – Start with your current high volume customers – Ask them questions.

Here is a sample script for Current Customers.

Hi _____, my name is _____from _____. Thank you for taking the time out of your busy schedule today to take my call. I was wondering if I could ask you a couple of questions. Do you have an email address?

_____, what is it that you like about our products or services?

In your opinion, what it is that I can do to improve my company or service to you?

Do you have a particular time of year that works best for you that we could sit down and plan out some promotions for you?

(Perhaps you could help him or her plan out what they would use for a special function, or an upcoming event.)

Ask if they have some employees that they would like to recognize for great performance.

Ask if they have a personal special occasion that they will need a personalized gift.

(You might just as well be the one to get that business! Let them talk and listen-Take Notes)

I am creating a way that will keep you informed of all of our new services, updates and any new products that we are carrying. I would like to invite you to visit our website at _____ and sign up for our_____. By doing so, you will be one of the first people that will have access to any of our specials!

(This would be your Automatic Emailing System & Blog-Invite them to visit your website and sign up for your FREE giveaway – I show you how to create this in the Embroidery Business Marketing System Program at www.EmbroideryBusinessMarketingSystem.com)

Is there any type of gifts or promotional products that you are looking for that you have not been able to find?

(Make sure that you listen to everything that they have to say. This is extremely important. Remember this is not a sales call. You are not trying to sell him anything, you are merely letting him know that you are here to help him with all of his gift giving ideas or needs.)

(If you are planning an event you can extend an invitation)

I would also like to invite you to an open House I will be holding showcasing many of our new products and services.

_____, We now have a Referral Program that would greatly benefit you.

(Tell them how the Referral program will benefit them)

Is it OK that I send you some business cards to hand out so that you can start reaping the benefits of our new program right away?

Thank you so much for taking time out of your busy day to chat with me for a few minutes.. I really appreciate it. Your input is really important to me. Have a great day!

After you are finished talking to them, send them a Thank You card with your Business Cards inside and also give them the link to your website/Blog that has your lead capture form on it.

(I show you how to create this in the Embroidery Business Marketing System Program www.EmbroideryBusinessMarketingSystem.com)

Here is a sample script for former or lost customers.

Hi _____, my name is _____from _____. Thank you for taking the time out of your busy schedule today to take my call. I was wondering if I could ask you a couple of questions.

_____, I know that you are no longer using us as your supplier for your gift items and promotional products. Is there a way that we can change that?

If you don't mind my asking, what was it that I did or did not do that made you decide to go elsewhere?

(If it is just price, you cannot do anything about this.)

Would you mind if I continued to keep in contact with you?

Do you have an email address?

I am creating a way that will keep you informed of all of our new services, updates and any new products that we are carrying. I would like to invite you to visit our website at _____ and sign up for our_____. By doing so, you will be one of the first people that will have access to any of our specials!

(This would be your Automatic Emailing System & Blog-Invite them to visit your website and sign up for your FREE giveaway – I show you how to create this in the Embroidery Business Marketing System Program at www.EmbroideryBusinessMarketingSystem.com)

(If you are planning an event you can extend an invitation)

I would also like to invite you to an open House I will be holding showcasing many of our new products and services.

_____, We now have a Referral Program that would greatly benefit you.

(Tell them how the Referral program will benefit them)

Is it OK that I send you some business cards to hand out so that you can start reaping the benefits of our new program right away?

Thank you so much for taking time out of your busy day to chat with me for a few minutes. I really appreciate it. Your input is really important to me. Have a great day!

After you are finished talking to them, send them a Thank You card with your Business Cards inside and also give them the link to your website/Blog that has your lead capture form on it.

(I show you how to create this in the Embroidery Business Marketing System Program www.EmbroideryBusinessMarketingSystem.com)

This handwritten thank you note will go a long way in helping to build your new customer relationship and it will be something that they will not forget!

Getting your customer's opinions and feedback is extremely valuable to your business and makes it a lot easier to plan your strategies as to how to work with them and provide them with the type of services and products that they will be anxious to purchase from you. They really do appreciate you asking them what they need. This can be the beginning of a long working relationship with each one of your customers.

Effective Way To Increase Sales By Hosting A Customer Appreciation Night

Hosting a Customer Appreciation Night is a fun and effective way to let your customers, friends, and family know that you are truly ready for business or you want to increase your business. Be creative in putting together your invitations and planning what specials you will have to offer. Encourage your guests to bring a friend with them.

Make sure the invitations are of the same high quality workmanship as your embroidery. It can be a Holiday Party theme, Wedding theme, Corporate theme, House Warming Party theme or a Sports theme, depending on your market niche. Let your guests know that they will receive a free gift just for attending. Create something embroidered for them to take home. This can be done very inexpensively.

If you are having a Holiday Party theme, you could make some felt ornaments. If it is a House Warming Party theme or a Wedding theme, you could purchase some inexpensive napkins. If you are having a corporate or sports theme, you could purchase some inexpensive caps. All of these items should be embroidered with your logo and contact information on them.

If you want to reach a certain niche market you could concentrate on that alone and create a theme that would be fitting just for them. If you are a retail business a Customer Appreciation Night can be held more than once during the course of the year, perhaps in January when business is slow and in the early fall to create holidays business.

Important Customer Appreciation Details

The best hours for these Customer Appreciation Nights are from 4 pm until 7 pm. This will give people a chance to come during business hours or after work. Holding the event for two nights usually works better than one night because more people will be able to fit one of the nights into their schedule.

If you have a home business, it can be held off premises. A small room in a hotel or a meeting room in a club or organization will work for this purpose.

If the Customer Appreciation Night is at your place of business, have your machines running. This is very impressive. You can be running the items that they are going to be taking home. Seeing the process actually done is very exciting to someone that does not know anything about embroidery.

Do not try to do this yourself if you are the only person in your business. See if you can pull in a helper and get them trained enough to run the one type of job, over and over for that night. This could be a son or daughter, husband or trusted friend. It is not hard to train someone to do this if they are only going to be doing the same job over and over.

You need to be free so that you can mingle and be talking to your customers and prospective customers. You want to be as helpful and answer as many questions as possible.

Gift Baskets – Great Gift Display Idea

Have a variety of different samples displayed in an attractive manner and encourage them to ask questions. Help them to visualize their ideas on a garment or other item. If this is a House Warming Party theme, have some gifts baskets made up for the different themes. You could have one made up for a bridal shower, one for a baby shower, one for a House Warming gift, one for a ladies birthday and even a child's birthday. These items are very easy to sell.

The gift baskets could contain various items but most of all, embroidered products. An example of products could be for a bridal shower, a bath towel, hand towel and washcloth set along with a roll of embroidered toilet paper and embroidered soap. They could all have the bridal couple's new monogram on them.

Keep It Simple

Have plenty of business cards and brochures for them to take. Make up a form for them to fill out with all of their contact information on it including their email address. Have a bowl or basket for them to drop this form into. You can have a drawing for a gift certificate at the end of the evening. Serve refreshments, but keep it simple. You want this to be a fun event for you and the guests.

A Customer Appreciation Night does not have to be expensive to be very effective. Keep it simple and most of all have fun and make sure that it is an event that your guests will remember. Remember, everyone needs personalized gift items, even your corporate clients. We all have Weddings to attend, birthdays, anniversaries and need gifts for many other occasions, personal and corporate.

The Most Efficient Way To Create
A Total Marketing System

Creating a web presence is a major part of any embroidery business. This is just as important to a local embroiderer as it is to one that is trying to reach the market globally. Before you can begin to reach a worldwide market, you must first reach out to your local market and the best and most cost effect way to do this is through your own web presence.

In today's economy your prospects want to learn all that they can about you and see what you have to offer before they will choose to do business with you. This has been brought about because of all of the Social Marketing that has taken place in the past couple of years. The entire marketing system has changed and the way that business has been marketing in the past has totally changed.

Everyone in business needs to create a web presence. Having a web site is very impressive to your customers and clients and if it is one that they can interact with, that is even better and means a lot more to them. This puts you at a whole new level in the eyes of your customers or clients. The best way to accomplish this is with a Blog and an automatic emailing program called an Autoresponder.

Creating your web presence with the Marketing System that I use is search engine optimized, very simple and easy to use and will get you up and running very quickly! This is very important, you do not have the time to go out and do research to find a system and then try to learn how to use it. You must get your marketing system going quickly!

(This marketing system can be found at EmbroideryBusinessMarketingSystem.com.)

You may already have a website but you are not receiving the amount of traffic or orders that you need to even cover the cost of the monthly website fees. This is unfortunate. Creating a website, no matter what system you are using, takes time. You may have paid a lot of money to have your site professionally built, or you may have had one set up for you by a friend. You may have even built your own using one of those template systems that are easy to purchase on the internet. Most of the template sites charge you by the month and the fees are determined according to however many products you are featuring on your site. There are some very expensive systems available that do a great job for you and are easy to keep up once you get them set up. The total system that I have created is very cost effective and has unlimited possibilities; however it is going to take a little time to get it all set up.

Do not ever make the mistake of getting into any type of free system, they absolutely do not work and you will get very frustrated when you are not receiving any traffic or sales from this type of system.

Components Of A Complete Marketing System

There are several components to a complete marketing system. When you are searching for the right package, the following components are necessary to complete your marketing system and get you ranked in the search engines.

- Homepage
- Marketing Pages
- Blog
- Automatic Emailing System
- Shopping Cart
- Social Media

Homepage

The Homepage is the front door to your business. You may also hear it referred to as a Squeeze page. It is a static page. What that means is that it does not change. It has basic information on it about your business and an offer. The purpose of your home page is to get the name and email address of a prospect that you can market to. You place a form on your homepage asking the customer to fill in their name and email address. In exchange for their name and email address, you will send to them some type of a gift, free report, article, coupon or tip of the week. You can even create a simple newsletter to send to them.

Marketing Pages

These are pages that you can create to market different items that you want to feature or even different niches. If you have more than one niche and do not want the products to be mixed, you can create separate marketing pages that will feature products designed just for that niche market.

Add a Testimonials Page to your site. This can be done with a Marketing page. This will show your prospects that you have a list of happy satisfied customers and will help to build confidence in you as a supplier for their promotional products.

Blog

What is a Blog? You are hearing that term more and more and yet no one really explains it to you. "Wikipedia" gives us a good definition.

"A Blog (a contraction of the term "Web log") is a web log usually maintained by an individual with regular entries of commentary, descriptions of events, or other material such as graphics or video. Entries are commonly displayed in reverse-chronological order."

A Blog is interactive, where as a regular website is not. This is the first website or part of your marketing system that you should create. It is an excellent tool and time saving way of keeping in constant contact with your customers. Your customers can forward your blog to their family, friends and or acquaintances to let them know what you are doing and what you have to offer. They can even make comments back to you about your entries or ask you questions about a product. You can send out quick notices to your customers letting them know that you are going to have a special or that you are adding a new product or service. If you keep a very friendly tone, your customers will really appreciate you keeping them informed.

With your Blog, you can easily add and change the pictures of your products and show your customers what you are featuring each month for your specials.

You can write articles on subjects that are applicable to your business and add them to your site. This is a very good way to attract new customers and the search engines as well. When you create a new post, it is indexed by the search engines and this helps to create your search engine rankings.

There are a lot of free article sites where you can find and download interesting articles and send them to your customers. You can even post tips and helpful hints.

If you already have a website, you still need to create a web presence with a Blog so that you can be more interactive with your customers. You cannot easily add this type of content to a website but within 5 minutes you can have a post ready and up on your Blog.

Many people think that all that they have to do is create a template website, put up one of those generic catalogs that all of the suppliers furnish and the people will find them quickly and purchase their products. Unfortunately this is not true. Most embroiderers do not see many orders for those websites. Your website needs to be optimized with keywords so that the search engines will crawl them and give you good ranking. This is not possible with most of those websites.

This is possible with a Blog. Each one of your posts, if it has good keywords in it, will get crawled by the search engines. It is so much easier to get a good ranking in the search engines with a Blog than it is with one of those template websites.

Automatic Emailing System

An Autoresponder is another term for an automatic emailing program. You can set up your messages and they will automatically be sent out to your customers as they subscribe to your free offer. When they subscribe they are placed into your emailing program. They will be sent out an email asking them to confirm that they have in fact requested your free offer. Then all of your follow up messages with be sent out to them whenever you schedule a mailing. It is a very set it and forget system. You can write one email and the system will personalize it with their name and it will send it out to everyone on your list at one time. A huge time saver!

You can prepare a series of emails, upload them to the system, tell the system which days you want them to go out to your customers and you do not have to think about it until you want to write another email. The Automatic emailing system that I have found that works great and has excellent email delivery is http://www.AutomaticEmailSystem. com.

Shopping Cart

This is the art of your website that will hold a listing, pictures, description, and pricing of each one of your individual products or services. This is the part of the marketing system that your customer will be directed to actually purchase your products or services. A shopping cart is hosted on a separate domain but is connected to your main marketing system. When your customer purchases a product they will then be sent a message from your emailing system and you will be able to follow up with them on a consistent basis and market your items to them through your automatic system.

Social Media

The last part of your Total Marketing System is Social Media. Social Media is everywhere today and we have to learn to embrace it. It is not going away any time soon and it has changed everything that we do in our business. It has changed how we set up our websites, how we market to our customers and even how we stay in touch with our customers.

Being able to connect all of your Social media together is a huge time saver and this is done by setting up a total social media system through your blog. Most of us have spent very little time thinking through how we really want to connect with our customers or even what we do to connect with them.

It is very important when you are planning out your system, how you position yourself in front of your market. This takes a lot of thought and planning but if you do that before you start setting up your system, you will save yourself a lot of time and effort. When I started setting up my Social Media sites I spent a lot of time redoing pages because of the lack of planning and it was a waste. Had I spent the time preplanning I could have avoided this.

You want to give and share good content more than you sell. It builds credibility when you create content on your blog and send it to **Facebook**, **Twitter** and **LinkedIn**. Do not try to sell from **Twitter**. You can create posts on your blog and they will automatically post on **Twitter**, **Facebook** and **LinkedIn**. You can also send out a broadcast email from your automatic emailing system that will post on all of the Social media networks if you have it configured to do so. This is really exciting and a huge timesaver.

There is software that can help you manage this, but do not use it until you have sent out a lot of tweets and interact often with your following. If you do decide to use software to manage your messages on your Social sites, you want to make sure that you are also adding messages directly into **Facebook** also without the use of this software. **Facebook** recognizes these messages sent through the software and they are not happy with it. Many of your messages will not even show up.

A Good Web Presence – Most Cost Effective Way To Advertise

It is so important to create a good web presence and it will really help to boost your sales. This is very inexpensive when it comes to the cost of advertising and so much more effective. This is a very efficient way of spending your advertising dollars. This system works for you on a constant basis and will give you a quick return for your money. You cannot count on that with any other type of advertising system.

There are free blogging programs that would allow you to market for less money but they are not as effective and many have advertising that will show up on your page. This can be discouraging and you just do not want to deal with this type of a system. You are trying to promote you and your business, not someone else's software, website or business.

There are less expensive autoresponders as well, and some are free, but they are not as dependable, and those lower priced systems have less customer support; sometimes no customer support at all. The system that I use offers great support and training. I found out a long time ago that customer support is by far the most important benefit that a company has to offer. You want your autoresponder continually prospecting for new customers and having a dependable automatic system set up will make this happen.

You cannot spend your valuable time messing with free or cheap programs, when it can be more effectively spent working on your business. When I first started I spent many hours trying to setup a system because I did not want to spend the money to have it done. I wasted a lot of good production time in the process.

I finally created a whole new marketing system that I use today, and have taught many other students to use as well and it is constantly bringing in new prospects. When I started seeing the results of this new marketing system, I was really exciting. Your website is always a work in progress so don't get hung up on the thought that it is not finished. It will never be finished and this is a good thing. Your site must be continuously changing and updated, especially in this world of Social Media, if you want to rank in the search engines. I have been doing a lot of studying and learning in depth about all of the Social Media networks and even better ways to optimize by blog. There is so much to learn and it is changing on a continuous basis.

I have created a program that will teach you step by step how to create your own embroidery business marketing system to market your embroidery business.

(You can find it at EmbroideryBusinessMarketingSystem.com)

Offering Customers Three Quality Choices Will Help To Increase Sales Dramatically!

Another way to increase customer sales dramatically with your existing customers is to offer them an alternative. Many times they do not need to have the best quality shirt for their promotion. Maybe they will be just as happy with a lower priced shirt.

I found that by giving my customers three choices in quality of products I could increase my sales and create a happy customer at the same time. I would not compromise on the quality of my embroidery, but maybe they would settle for a Stock embroidery font rather than the digitized lettering in a logo. This could make a significant difference in the price of their one time set up. It would not change the running time of the design but between the price of a lower quality shirt or cap and the lower price of the initial set up, you could save the customer many dollars on the total order. I always gave my customer three quality choices.

A-Lesser Quality – Low level price

B-Average Quality – Mid level price

C-High Quality – High level price

I have followed this formula for all of my sales.

I always asked the customer what type of budget we were working with before I ever showed him or her any garments. I had them show me the logo and then I would go over what could be done and what I could do for him to meet their budget. At that point, I would show the customer the products in the price level that would fit within this budget. You gain their confidence immediately when you show them that you are willing to work with them to meet their particular needs. This method will work 99% of the time to increase your sales.

If a customer came in with a certain product in mind; that meant that he had been shopping elsewhere and was looking for a lower price. I was always up front with them and told them that if they were here shopping for a lower price that I probably would not be able to help them, but I would show him what I had and go through the exact same process. Sometimes what I had was better quality than what was already offered. A good percentage of the time the customer would go with my suggestions and work with us instead of continuing to shop around.

You cannot waste your time with customers that are only shopping for price. If they tell you that you have to beat someone else's price, let them go immediately, do not even start to work with them. This is a waste of the time that you could be spending on more productive work. You are in business to make a living; you are not running a charity!

Low Cost Methods Of Prospecting For New Customers

There are several methods that you can use to prospect for new customers. You can pay to advertise or you can attract prospects for free. I have always been very partial to the FREE end of advertising for obvious reasons. Besides the fact that it is FREE, you usually will find better prospects using the Free methods. That has been my experience in the past.

- Networking Off Line And On-Line
- Donate Products & Services To Charity For Fund Raising Events
- Ask For Referrals
- Attend Trade Shows In Your Niche
- Offer To Trade Your Products & Services
- Press Releases

In the past I spend a lot of money on advertising only to find out that most of the time it did not work the way that I expected it to. The newspaper was the most expensive method I ever tried and I never once received the results that I was looking for. I never even broke even on my investment.

The only paid advertising that ever worked for me were TV ads and they are not free, but I did trade my products and services for the advertising and that made it very low cost. In today's market you can use the trade dollars to advertise on websites at a lower cost than actually running an ad on the TV. Your name is displayed for a longer period and can be seen over and over again.

There are so many ways to prospect for new customers and many opportunities to make connections with people in all areas of your life. If you keep your eyes and ears wide open, you will find a gold mine right in front of you!

Always Wear Your Work

Every place that you go, you want to make sure that you have your business cards or brochures with you. Always wear your own embroidery work when you attend these functions and any other time that you can. Your work speaks in volumes so make sure that it is excellent at all times. Do not wear rejects.

Always make it a point to meet new people and ask for them for 2 business cards. One for yourself and one to pass along to someone else that might be looking for their services. On the back of the business card that you will keep, write down some notes about the person to help you remember them. Always follow up and thank them for the time that they took to talk to you. You can even send them a simple note or thank you card. This is very effective.

Networking – Fastest Way To Gain More Customers

Networking is one of the easiest and fastest ways to gain new customers and increase your customer sales. Networking takes a lot of work and time but the payoff is huge! Networking is for every area of your personal and business life. You must get into the habit of talking to everyone that you meet. You do not always have to talk about your business. You want to talk about the other person and listen to them and make friends before you promote your business. When you do talk about your business make sure that you are doing so in such a way that will benefit the other person.

You also want to be promoting non-competing services and products. If you can connect two people to each other through your networking, you are remembered and they will come to you when they are ready for your services. This is an excellent way to get started.

There are two types of networking, On line and Off line. Both types of networking are very important to your business!

On Line Networking

In today's marketplace it is very important to have a presence on the social networking sites. You cannot be physically present, but you can make many friends and acquaintances through these social networking sites. The three main ones that I have found to be the most useful are **Facebook**, **Twitter** and **LinkedIn**. You can join them, create your profile and establish a following. There are new ones popping up all of the time, but Facebook is the giant of all of the social media sites today.

After you have created a following you can promote your business through these social sites. With **Facebook** you can create a Business page and join a local group in your own community. **Facebook** is an excellent tool to use for networking. **Facebook** and **LinkedIn** are used primarily for business. You should make personal acquaintances first before you start promoting your business. You will have better results if you promote on a personal level.

(In my Embroidery Business Marketing System,
www.EmbroideryBusinessMarketingSystem.com
I show you how to set up a Business Page on Facebook.)

Off Line Networking

There are many organizations that you can join but the main ones are the local Chamber of Commerce and a Women's or Men's Business

Organization. There are also networking groups that meet for lunch in many areas.

If you join an organization, you must become active. You will have the opportunity to meet key people and this will help with your credibility. Just joining the organization does no good if you do not make yourself known to the other members. When they have functions, you must attend. The **Chamber of Commerce** in our area has an early morning Breakfast and an After Hours mixer once a month.

The breakfasts are held at a local hotel and they always have a guest speaker. I have found these breakfast functions very informative. The After Hours mixer is held at one of the local member's establishment and you are encouraged to bring business cards or brochures and of course mingle and talk to the other guests. Each month one member is invited to bring in a sample display of their products or services to show the other members. I have learned a lot by attending these functions and gained many customers.

The networking groups that meet for lunch usually limit it to one company of a type of business for each industry. Only one person can join that has an embroidery business. There are no competitors allowed. This has also been very lucrative for me.

Networking is a way of life, and we should be utilizing it more in our business life. Networking and the opportunity to network is everywhere. Always carry your business cards and let everyone know that you are in business, what you do and most importantly, what you can do for them.

Give your friends and family members several business cards and ask them to give them to their acquaintances. Everyone that you meet must know what you do and what you have to offer!

Donate Products/Services For Fund Raising

Charity and organizations are always looking for Fund Raising ideas. They depend on the donations of business to help defray their costs. Donating your products or services is an excellent low cost way for you to help them meet their obligations and in return you have the opportunity to gain new customers.

You will also receive a great deal of publicity and gain the attention of a many key people.

If at all possible have your logo as part of the product. If not directly on the product, then create a tag and attach it to the product. This is an excellent way to get your name out in front of a lot of people. Your name and contact information is usually listed in the program that is being provided by the organization.

I have a student that has been very successful with fund raising events by donating the embroidery on shirts that organizations have purchased from him at cost. He embroiders their logo on the left chest and his logo on the sleeve. He attaches a tag to each garment with his contact information on it. He has been able to raise the awareness of his business with his logo being seen over and over. His products are always very high quality and he has gained a lot of new customers using this strategy.

Another fund raising idea that is of no cost to you, is selling your finished products and services to clubs and organizations, and give them back a percentage of your profits. This works great for school booster clubs and church youth groups that are trying to raise money for a particular project. I have a student that is very successful with this strategy. She sells her products during school events and gives back to the school organization a percentage of her profits. For this strategy, you would not be allowed to add your logo, but you can still attach a card to the garment containing your logo and contact information.

There are many ideas and opportunities for fund raising within your own community. Check with the local **Chamber of Commerce** for a list of fund raising opportunities in your area. This is a great way for you to give back to the community and at the same time raise the awareness of what your business has to offer. Donating is always a great way to gain new customers.

Set Up A Referral Program To Increase Your Customer Base

Setting up a Simple Referral Program for your Embroidery Business takes only a few minutes and is so worth it. Asking for referrals is one of the most effective, quickest and least expensive ways of gaining new customers. Setting up a system to reward customers for referrals by giving them a discount on their next order is always effective. There are several ways of asking for referrals. **The key here is ASKING for a referral.** Many people think that this goes without saying, if someone likes your product, they will pass on the word. This is not always true. Everyone is busy and they do not think of spreading the word about you. You must make a point of always asking and find creative ways of getting those referrals.

- Have Business cards Tucked into Customers Pick Up Bags.
- Send out Business Cards or Brochures with Invoices.
- Ask for a Referral after Customer has placed their order.
- Tell Employees about your Referral Program

Have Business Cards Tucked Into Customers Pick Up Bags

The easiest and most effective way that I found was to always give my customers business cards and brochures. When they pick up their order, make sure to add a business card or brochure to their package. Ask them to write their names on the back of the cards or brochures and hand them to their friends, family and acquaintances. When the person comes into the shop that has been referred, take their business card and keep track of the person that referred them to you. The person that gave the referral would then get a discount on their next order. Everyone wants to get something for giving out your name. As I said there is a small cost to it, but this is a customer that you did not have to go after.

Send Out Business Cards Or Brochures With Invoices

This is another easy way to get referrals. As a general rule, they will tuck the business cards in their wallet and will hand them out when someone asks about their embroidery. Make sure that they know that they must put their name on the back of the cards so that they can get a discount on their next order.

Ask For A Referral After Customer Has Placed Their Order

Ask if they have a friend or acquaintance that may be in the market for their services. Perhaps it is a holiday time and they may be looking for a gift item. This is always an easy time to find new customers when you are asking for referrals. You can then call that referral and let them know that Mr. or Mrs. (your customer) was in your shop looking for a special gift and you thought maybe they would also be in the market for a special gift for a loved one for the holiday. This could be for Valentine's Day, Mothers Day, Fathers Day, Easter, an Anniversary, Wedding, Christmas or any other special time of the year.

Keeping Track of the Referrers

I set up a simple spreadsheet for my Referral program. On that spreadsheet, I put the Date, Customers Name, Name of Referrer, Amount of Sale, Date Referrer Purchased after Referring and Amount of Referrer's Sale. This helps me to keep track of the amount of sales that are brought in by the Referrers and who the Referrers are. You can increase the reward for those that give you a lot of referrals. This is the best type of Salespeople that you can have!

Tell everyone that you know about your Referral Program including your employees. This is a simple way to set up a Referral program for your Embroidery Business that WORKS!

I have a copy of the Referral Program Spreadsheet that I use. You can download it from my website and use it to keep track of your Referrers.

(Embroiderybusinesssuccess.com/set-simple-referral-program-embroidery-business-works/)

A Good Tool For Prospecting Is To Attend Niche Market Trade Shows

If you have a niche market or you have a niche market that you are contemplating on pursuing, attend as many trade shows as possible in that market niche. I do not mean niche market trade shows to look for products to sell; I mean trade shows in which you are looking for prospects to sell to. Every market niche has some type of event, or function where they have a display of their products or services. There are shows in the shopping malls through out the year for different types of organizations or industry. This is also true of your local county fairs.

Niche Market Trade Shows offer three types of contacts.

1. Show Producers

2. Vendors

3. Attendees

Market To Show Producers

There are opportunities marketing to the producers of the Niche Market Trade Show. They need apparel for their employees, bags to give away for the attendees to use, badges and signage. This is an opportunity to trade your products or services or free space as a vendor.

The Vendors are excellent prospects. At first, you do not have to be there as vendor or an exhibitor yourself. Just go to mingle with the people and talk to the people behind the tables or the vendors, whichever is applicable Talking to the people behind the tables is easy and many times you can create a customer out of them. These are always good prospects for display items or promotional products that they can use to give away.

Exhibit Your Own Products

If you have settled on a niche market, you can go as an exhibitor and show your own products. Before the event opens, you want to make sure that you visit as many other vendors as possible to let them know what you have to offer. This is a good place to pick up new customers and prospective customers. Approach them by telling them something positive about their display or appearance. This is very important. You want to be as friendly and open as possible.

Make sure that you are wearing your own apparel with you company logo on it. That speaks volumes. It is a lot easier to convince someone that you have a quality product when you are actually displaying it on yourself. It is also best to have a high quality product on rather than a mediocre one for this purpose. As a general rule the embroidery on a higher quality garment will be more striking that on a lower quality garment.

You also want to have plenty of business cards, postcards or brochures to hand out. Many times postcards are even better than a business card for a trade show because you have more space for your message.

Give the vendor your print material and tell how they can benefit from using you as a supplier of their products. If they already have a supplier, offer them a discount coupon to give you a chance at their business and make sure that you tell them about your referral program. This is a very good hook for this type of customer. They are usually very happy to refer other people to you as well.

Items that vendors need for display purposes are banners, table skirts, staff shirts or small promotional give away items. Many times you can find the names of the exhibitors before the show and call them up to let them know that you can help them with their display needs.

If they already have their display items for the upcoming show, ask them if they know of any other vendors that you could contact about their needs and tell them about your referral program.

Working With Attendees

If you are not exhibiting, just attending, you can talk to people after they leave the vendors tables. I have created many customer relationships by talking to people that walked away from the exhibitors and offered my services if the conversation was applicable. Listening to these conversations gives you a wealth of information. You have to be careful when you are using this tactic because you can be asked to leave the event if you are caught soliciting the attendees when you are not an exhibitor. You want to be discreet and friendly. Make sure that you have your print materials in a bag and not out so that everyone can see them.

These types of shows offer many opportunities that you should be taking advantage of.

Low Cost Tool For Gaining New Customers Is Trading Products Or Services

Trading your products and services to another business is another great way to increase your awareness and your customer sales. If you want to increase your awareness through advertising, trading your products and or services to the media is an excellent way to do this, but you must be careful that you come out a winner in this deal.

When you are trading products or services you always want to charge the other person or business a retail price, not your wholesale or organizational price. They are charging you retail, so please keep that in mind. It has to be at your advantage or this will not work for you.

In today's market you can use trade dollars to advertise on TV station's websites at a lower cost than actually running an ad on the TV or radio. This is very effective for one of my private coaching clients. He even picked up a new customer from a national network as a result of his ads being seen on the local TV station's website.

Another type of trade that works great is carpentry work, book keeping or a delivery service. You can trade their services for your products. This type of trade is always good for referrals. I have been able to use trade to bring in several new customers.

I have traded services with my accountant and I even traded my Chamber of Commerce dues in exchange for a banner.

Trading your products and services is always a good way to get your name out in front of people.

Marketing – Keep It Simple

Your Marketing Plan does not have to be complicated. Keep it as simple as you possibly can. The main points of marketing are; to build relationships with your current customers, create an on-line presence, and network to find new customers. It really is as simple as that. It does take time, but you must start today and get into the habit of providing the highest quality customer service that you can possibly provide. If you do, it will increase your steady flow of current customers and they will in turn refer new customers to your embroidery business!

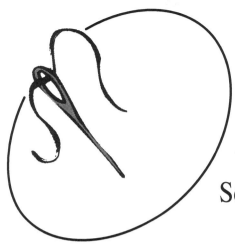

#3
Knowing How
To Price
Your Products Or
Services For Profit

"Annual income twenty pounds, annual expenditure nineteen six, result happiness. Annual income twenty pounds, annual expenditure twenty pound ought and six, result misery."

~Charles Dickens~

Pricing Your Products Or Service Correctly Is An Art That You Must Develop Quickly!

Starting your embroidery business is exciting and many times it is the result of a dream! You have a strong desire to be creative and provide special gift items or products to your family, friends, neighbors, and new customers; but you cannot do this without charging a fair price for your creativity and the time that you spend in creating these items. Trying to figure out what you should actually charge is one of the main concerns that most embroiderers have when they are first starting out in business. This concern does not change after they have been in business for a while and are trying to run a profitable business.

Pricing is an art that must be developed for your business and your niche market. Most embroiderers start out gathering price lists from other embroiderers, competitors or other people that they know that have started their own embroidery business. They will then develop their price list according to what everyone else is charging.

No two embroiderers have the same expenses or circumstances and it is impossible to work with someone else's price list and expect that you are going to make a profit.

New embroiderers and even many seasoned embroiderers do not know where to begin when it comes to pricing their embroidery. For some reason this is a subject that is very scary and it is easier to work with someone else's pricing than trying to develop your own.

How I Really Struggled With Pricing

Pricing is the one area that I spend a lot of time on when I am working with my private clients. I truly understand why it is so hard for a new embroiderer to get this part of their business right.

I really struggled with pricing. I had enough work; worked long hours and yet I was not making a profit. I could not understand what I was doing wrong. My accountant told me that I need to start keeping track of every movement that I made in that shop. At first I thought he was crazy, there was no way that I could do that. He helped me to develop some spreadsheets that I could use to get me started timing every step. My employees were really having fits because they looked at it as paperwork. They did not want to do any paperwork, they hated paperwork! They wanted to embroider. Once I got then into the habit and I had to force the issue, I was shocked at what I discovered. I was giving away all of my work and absolutely not making any money at all. I created my price list like everyone else did, I used other peoples and then did an average and that was my price!

After I had gone through a period of time keeping track of everything that actually went into a job, I decided along with the help of my accountant to raise my prices. I was scared to death to do this, but I had no choice! Either raise the prices or go out of business! I could not do that, I had 32 employees at the time and that was a huge responsibility.

I was afraid that I would lose all of my customers. What happened was, I did lose some of them, but they were people that were working with us because of price alone. The ones that were interested in high quality stayed and I rebuilt from there. This was the beginning of not working so hard to bring in enough to pay the bills. I was not even taking a salary before I started my new pricing structure. After that, my accountant insisted that I started taking a salary every week. He said that this was no way to run a business! He was right! It was a small one to start with but it was at least something and it made me feel so much better knowing that I was also going to get a paycheck at the end of the week.

I work with embroiderers all the time that do not take a salary. It is not fun to work so hard and not get paid! There is a specific structure that you need to go through in order to develop your own pricing system that will work in all areas of your business. This is very important!

Let Go Of The Myths Of Pricing
That Will Create A Trap For You

The first part of creating your own pricing structure is to let go of all of the myths that you have heard in the past about pricing. You have to remember, you are in this business to make money; you are not in business just to survive! Sometimes, it seems like that is the scenario that we are in, especially in today's economy, but we must change that.

These 7 myths that you must forget are:

- My prices must be lower than the competition!
- Cost plus desired profit margin is the final selling price!
- Low prices will create loyalty!
- I have money coming in every day, it pays the bills!
- Drop your prices if sales are lagging!
- I just started my business; my prices have to be lower so that I can get the work!
- With my new software I can create designs faster so I do not have to charge as much!

Believing in or following any of these myths will choke the life out of your business! You cannot work with prices lower than the competition, there is no loyalty when it comes to pricing in this business, you do not drop your prices if sales are lagging, and most of all, you do not price your products lower so that you can get the work! All of these will lead to the death of your business.

Unfortunately this is how so many embroiderers start their business. They have no idea that this is not the right way to get started. They just figure if they gather all of the price lists from the competitors and then come up with an average that they should be good. "I hear over and over, I have to keep my prices this low or I do not get any work, but I am struggling trying to pay my bills!"

If you feel like you are in that trap, I understand. I have been there also, but you must break those chains and start creating a pricing structure that will give you a profit or get out of business. You will eventually lose your business anyway if you continue down this same path. That is the same situation I was in before my accountant helped to rescue me.

I worked with a large customer that was caught in the trap of lowering his prices thinking that it would create loyalty. All it did was bring in a lot of work that he could not handle. He had to hire and train new employees, incurring another expense, just to be able to handle the work load. It sounds like that would be a good deal, but actually all it did was drive down his profit margin and create more expense for him because of errors made by new or untrained employees. This is a trap you want to avoid at all costs!

Developing A Total Pricing Structure

You must first develop a total pricing structure that will work in whatever situation that you are faced with. This is the first step before you can create the actual price list. This could be for the retail market, school market, corporate market, wholesale market or whatever market or business situation that you are working in. Your pricing structure must work and be flexible to cover each of these markets and readily adapt to change. Pricing is not as scary as it seems if you take into consideration all of the factors that go into doing business. What are some of those factors?

- Overhead costs
- Product Costs and Markup
- Market Niche
- Type of services that you perform
- Your geographical location

There is also the factor of perceived value. Many products or items of service can be marked up higher than others because of the perceived value, such as a cap. A cap can be marked up 2 or 3 times what the cost is to you, but you would generally not mark up an expensive jacket or golf shirt 2 or 3 times unless of course you were in that type of market niche.

The large successful companies know what their costs are and develop concrete pricing structures that are required to maintain their level of profitability.

This is not always easy for a small company or a home based embroiderer to grasp, but it is no different for you. You too must develop a concrete pricing structure and stick with it. Without this type of pricing structure you will not grow or even survive. Up until now you may have been doing embroidery for your friends and family. If you charged them anything, it was probably a very small charge. Now you want to start charging what you are actually worth and it is tough to make that transition but it is a very necessary one if you are serious about having a successful embroidery business.

Everyone has different wants, needs, expenses, markets, situations and equipment. Your formula must be created using your numbers and yours alone. You cannot charge according to what the business across town is charging. Many embroiderers make this mistake and do not stay in business very long because they are not making a profit.

Does anyone have a magic formula? I know that there must be one out there or something basic that we can follow, right? Wrong!

There have been many articles written about pricing in the trade magazines and every article has a different approach but it always boils down to the fact that you have to know what your true costs are each and every month before you can begin to establish a good pricing structure.

How Do I Start Developing My Pricing Structure?

There are specific steps that you must follow in creating your pricing structure. Knowing what all of your expenses are is the very first step. Your entire pricing structure will be based on your figures and your figures alone.

- Create a spread sheet of all your business related expenses
- Create Cost Analysis Spread Sheet
- Create A good work flow organization
- Keep track of production times
- Keep track of design set up times
- Keep track of Machine Production times
- Create A Price List Prep Sheet
- Create Your Price List
- Create Corporate Price List for apparel

Create A Spread Sheet Of All Business Expenses

Gather all of your expenses for your business and lay them out on a spread sheet in a spread sheet program such as Microsoft Excel or Open Office Calc. If you do not have Excel, you can download Open Office for Free at http://www.openoffice.org. It works just the same as Excel.

Make sure that you list all of your business expenses and you must include your salary or the salary that you want to make, and your home expenses for the area that you are using. Do not skimp on this if you are operating your business from your home. The base of your pricing structure must be developed to give you the profit to help you with future growth. You will need to figure this for each month and then for the year. This way you can work with an average number for your Total Cost Analysis Spread Sheet.

If you paid cash for your embroidery machine, you still want to include a machine payment. You need to have that built into your formula so that you can set money aside for your next machine.

One mistake many embroiderers make when they are operating their business from their home is to think that they have no overhead so they leave all of these figures out when they are creating their expense spread sheets. This is the wrong approach right from the beginning. You must include those expenses just as if you were paying rent and all of the expenses of your utilities when you are creating this first step. If you do not have all of these figures plugged in, you will not be creating a true picture or one that will allow you to grow and set aside money for the future.

Separate your expenses for the different areas of your business. If you are doing screen printing, digital printing or sewing custom twill and neither process is part of embroidery, then these expenses must be removed from the spread sheet for embroidery. You are only using the expenses that are associated with embroidery for creating your embroidery pricing.

You will need to do the same process to figure pricing for the other areas of your business. This is the only accurate way to get the true picture of what you should be charging for each area. The process works exactly the same, and you can use all of the same formulas, but you must have separate and accurate figures for arriving at each of your price lists.

Create A Total Cost Analysis Spread Sheet

After you have all of your expenses calculated, you will then figure out how many days a year that you are actually running your embroidery business, how many hours a day you run your machine, how many minutes an hour your machine is running, how many machine heads you are running, and your machine speed. You will be able to calculate the actual cost of each stitch and your breakeven point. This is extremely important. Without these figures, you cannot possibly produce a price list that is going to make you any profit. This total cost analysis is very important in your overall financial plan for your business. If you have created your formal business plan with your projections, you will have all of this information. I have a Total Cost Analysis Spread Sheet included in my **"How To Develop A Profitable Price List For Today's Market Place"** embroidery pricing program.

(www.HowToPriceEmbroidery.com)

Creating A Good Work Flow Organization

Creating and maintaining a good work flow organization with both your embroidery processes and paper work is extremely important to any sized embroidery organization. Take the time out to see exactly how your work is flowing through your embroidery shop. Is the lack of a good work flow system costing you time and money?

I was recently working with a company that has been in the embroidery business for many years, but has recently been sold. This is a medium sized company with several multi-head embroidery machines that creates a top quality finished product!

The new owners are… keeping the same management in place, wanted to increase their embroidery production flow using all of the same equipment that is currently in production with no plans for any new equipment purchases in the near future. This can be done, but first a new organization plan must be put into effect. By that I mean a work flow organization that also includes a change in the paper work flow and some of the current production processes.

After reviewing many of the current processes I found that a lot of time is wasted in their movements during each of the processes and going from one process to another. It is extremely important to know exactly how much time it takes to do every single step within the entire manufacturing or embroidery process.

This process starts at the exact moment that an order is taken and continues through all of the steps of planning and manufacturing right up until it is billed. Each one of these steps has a time and cost associated with it. The work flow should be time studied at each stage of development to see if there is another way or movement that can be changed or incorporated to help the process be done faster and more efficiently. It is very important to keep track of each one of these steps in the total process.

I have found that in most cases there is not enough thought put into the planning process before each step. This is especially important as a small embroidery business is growing and expanding into a larger organization.

Start Timing All Of Your Production And Artwork Jobs

Until you actually start the process of timing your jobs and all of the movements and processes that go into each job, you do not realize all of the time that is wasted on each job. This is a huge step in learning exactly what goes into each job and what it is actually costing you.

I have a Production Tracking & Timing sheet that I use to track each one of my jobs. It starts with taking the order all of the way through to shipping the package out of the door. Each second and minute of your time is costing you money. Each second and minute of your employees' time is costing you money. You must know where all of those seconds and minutes are going. Use a stop watch or a time clock to start timing all of your jobs.

Do you have any idea as to what it is costing you or your employee to take an order from a customer? Do you know exactly how much it is costing you to hoop 1 garment or fold and package your garments for shipping? Each one of these processes or movements must be tracked so that you know. These processes are all part of your pricing structure. This is not hard, but it does take some time and practice to get used to.

Once you start keeping track of the time for each process, you will start to find ways of cutting down those times or extra movements, and you begin to see real progress. When you first start, you are shocked at what each one is really costing you, but as I said, you soon learn how to cut corners and speed up the processes.

Keeping track of your processes goes for artwork and setting up your designs as well. This is another shocker. You set up your jobs because they need to be done, but you really do not know how much it is costing you to do so, and if you are including those sets ups FREE of charge, you realize very quickly that this is a huge mistake. All of those setups need to be charged to the customer.

The same is true if you are sending out your designs to a digitizer. You have time into each one of those designs before you actually send it to the digitizer. You have to figure how this design is going to be done, what colors go into it, what size it must finish and what type of fabric it is going to be sewn onto. When the design comes back, you then must stitch it out before you actually embroider it onto the garment. This takes time also. You need to add a profit onto the price that the digitizer charged you for that design. You cannot absorb all of those charges. They must be passed onto the customer.

Production Time Costs Money

Production time costs money and if your machine is not running, you are not making any money. That is how most embroiderers create their entire pricing structure. Their price lists are created around their stitch count for running the designs. What about all of the other time that goes into producing that order? Who pays for that part of getting the job done? You as the embroiderer are paying for that. Does that make any sense to you? It doesn't to me! The customer needs to be paying for that also. All of the rest of the production time needs to be considered into that price also.

Can I still charge by the stitch count? Sure you can if you add the extra time into that price for all of the other expenses. What do I mean by that? When you are timing your jobs, you will discover that it takes time for the machine to stop and change colors. Each color stop and change is about the same as embroidering 50-80 stitches. This all depends on the speed of your machine. Add that amount of time for each color change to your stitch count figure. What about trims? Same thing, you need to add extra stitches in your pricing structure to allow for the time it takes to do your trims.

Machine Production Schedule

I have a **"Machine Production Schedule"** that I created that has all of these values built into it. All I have to do to figure my actual machine production time is to put in my stitch count, number of garments, my machine speed, number of color changes & trims, and then my total production time is automatically figured out for me. I know exactly how many hours of embroidery I have in house at all times. This is an excellent planning tool as well as knowing how much can and should be produced each day.

Price List Prep Sheet

Our next step in creating your pricing structure is to create a Price List Prep Sheet. This sheet is a combination of your Machine Production Schedule and your Production Timing Sheet taken from your actual production timing. This will give you a true picture of what your costs are for each stitch count category and how much of a profit you can add. You can add whatever you want to create the profit margin that you want, but if you are quoting on a job and have to stay within a certain range, you can see immediately if this is possible.

This is another great tool that works for me flawlessly. If I need to change my profit point in order to get a job that I want, I can see within seconds if this is possible. If I cannot make a profit on a job, I do not take it. There is no point in changing money from one hand to another without making a profit on it. That does not make any sense for your business. It would be better to spend time working on something else that can make you money.

Price List

After my Price List Prep Sheet is finished, I can create my price list. Creating the price list is a process that only takes a few minutes after all of your other calculations are done. This will truly give you a price list that will make you a profit.

Without going through these processes, you are short of shooting in the dark hoping to make money. I have been there and I have had all of the bad experiences of not making any money when I thought that I was. It was a shock to me to see exactly what I was losing on each job. I had no idea as to what to do to get out of my rut, but working closely with my accountant and teaching him what I was really going through to get to the bottom line was the beginning of a whole new world for me!

He helped me create spread sheets and formulas to start my timing process. I improved upon them many times until I finally have a total system that really works great!

Corporate Apparel Price List With Embroidery

The last step in completing your Profitable Price list is to create a Corporate Apparel Price List that includes your embroidery pricing. You want to be able to give your customer a price instantly whether in your shop or out on location in the customer's presence. I created a format that included the embroidery price along with the apparel price.

The key to your price list is to keep it simple. First start with the cost of the apparel that you want to carry, add the shipping and then the percentage of markup that you are looking for.

The process that I use to arrive at a selling price is, I add the cost of the shipping to the cost of the item. I figure what I want as my percentage of markup. I then multiply my percentage of markup by the total cost of my item for the final selling price.

I start with a 2-5 category and then I add other quantity categories with discounts. In the format that I have created, I have formulas built in so that when I change the cost of the item, the list will automatically be updated. This may sound confusing to you, but it really is quite simple.

Below is a simplified version of my formula.

Formula: cost of item +cost of shipping = total cost

Desired markup * (times) total cost = final selling cost

Shirt 6.00 +3.50 shipping = 9.50 total cost.

Markup: 150% 1.50*9.50 = 14.25 selling price

I then add the price of the embroidery.

I have used 150% as my markup with this being a 50% markup. In your business you may need to add 200% or 125% for your markup. It all depends on your market, your niche and whatever markup it is that you need to cover all of your expenses and make a profit. The profit must be substantial enough that you will be paying yourself a salary and laying money aside for future growth. You must be constantly planning for future growth or your business will be at a standstill and you will not be able to add new products, procedures, processes or equipment.

In the system that I created all of the spreadsheets are linked together so that if you change any of your cost information in your **Cost Analysis Spread Sheet**, it will automatically update your **Prices List Prep Sheet**, your **Embroidery Price List**, and your **Corporate Price List**. This is a huge timesaver and will provide you with updated price lists at all times.

The **Corporate Price List** includes your items that you purchase with the markup of your choosing and the embroidery pricing for each category. I have created four **Stitch Count** categories, **A-B-C-D**, for each **Quantity of Pieces** categories. This cuts down on a lot of individual figuring of prices and is another huge timesaver. This way you can always be prepared for an instant price quote

You must create a different price list for retail, organizations and wholesale. This is done simply by changing the percentage of your markup for each type of sale. Your retail would be your full markup, your wholesale would be your lowest markup and your organizations would be some place in the middle of the two markups. This is done very quickly by just changing those numbers and printing out a new sheet.

Using Categories For Simple Customer Pricing

I created hang tags for my sample garments with the **A-B-C-D** prices written on the hang tags. This made pricing very easy. Before I visited a customer for a presentation, I had a phone conversation with them and knew exactly what they were looking for. I prepared my samples accordingly. This will make the presentation go quickly. I also took extra items or more expensive items to try and increase the sale. Again, if you have to come down a little to get the sale, you have already created room in your price list to give you that room.

The **Cost** of the item is your cost from the manufacturer or the distributor. I always use the piece price in my calculations. If you are in a situation where you are bidding against someone else, you can always add the dozens price instead if that is what it takes but I would not create my basic price list using anything other than the piece price. You can tell them how special they are and for them you are willing to give them a discount.

The **Percentage of Markup** will determine how much you want to make on the markup of your items. If you are selling to someone that is going to resell the items, then you will use a lower markup than you will if you are strictly selling to retail. This is your choice. You can choose any markup that you want to work with. You can go as low as 5% for your markup and still make money but I would not go any lower than that. You do not want to lose any money.

Between the markup of your items and the markup of your embroidery, you have many choices and can work within any type of situation. You have total control and flexibility with this type of format.

Learn How To Price And Make Adjustments

Knowing how to price your embroidery for profit is one of the most important elements in starting and running your embroidery business. If you do not know how to create a profit you will not be in business very long and all of your efforts will have been in vain.

Learning how to price really is not hard, but it takes a lot of time to get your total system together and know for sure that you are creating that profit. You must always time each and every order than comes into your place of business. I have been at this embroidery game for over 30 years now and I still time myself as I work through each and every job! Products change, fabrics change, the way that we go through our processes can change and you must keep up on all of those changes in order to have a success embroidery business. You must continually revisit your price list to make sure that your pricing is still making you that profit. If you do not make adjustments as you go along, you may be losing money and may not be aware of it..

(To create your own Embroidery Pricing Structure quickly, go to HowToPriceEmbroidery.com This program teaches you step by step how to time each of your processes and create your own Pricing Structure. It has many formatted spreadsheets already prepared for you to easily create your own price list, one that will help you make a profit!)

#4
Carve Out
Your Own
Niche Market

*I don't know the key to success, but the key to failure
is trying to please everybody.*

Bill Cosby
US comedian
& television actor (1937 -)

Branding Yourself A Specialist In A Specific Market Is Very Important!

There are two questions that many embroiderers asked on a regular basis about niche marketing. This is a term that is used over and over and to the new embroiderer, this can be a very confusing term.

• What is Niche Marketing?

• How do I find a niche market?

Niche marketing is marketing your product or service to a certain group or segment of the population. By creating or finding a solution to answer a unique need in that segment you can develop your entire business around that certain group or segment.

How do I find a niche market? The answer is, you do not find a niche market, you create or carve out a niche market!

It is hard to survive in today's marketplace competing for the same business that every other embroiderer is competing for. The average embroiderer starts out working in the corporate market offering hats, golf shirts, t-shirts, sweatshirts, jackets etc. because this is the easiest area to start. They soon find out that this is a tough market to compete in and every embroiderer in their local area is fighting for the same business. You must find an area of the market that you can specialize in; one that other embroiderers have overlooked or aren't willing to service. In this way, you can brand yourself as the specialist for that specific market.

You can quickly become the leader in your chosen market and will have less competition if you market to a specific niche rather than trying to compete with the masses.

How One Student Almost Quit Before She Found Niche Marketing

One of my students, was trying to market to everyone, which is the mistake most embroiderers make when they first get started, and she found herself running in circles and could not focus on any one thing. She was constantly trying to figure out how to market to all of these people. She paid someone to create quite an elaborate website for her. In her website she had one of those catalog sites that you can link to your site. She also had samples of her work but there was really no way for anyone to order her embroidery off of the site. They could order the products but then they had to call her to place an order for the embroidery.

She was paying this webmaster a monthly fee to host her site and it was not producing anything for her. Long story made short, she did not get any orders from that website. She ran an ad in the newspaper and since she was basically the new embroiderer in town, it was doing nothing but costing her money. She was ready to give up because her business was costing her way too much money and she just could not afford to keep up with the payment's on her machine.

She called me and wanted to know what she should do and how she could go about selling her machine. Prior to this phone call, I did not know this embroiderer. She found me on the web and thought that I might know of someone that could take the machine and payments off of her hands.

After listening to her story, I told her that she needed to focus her marketing efforts on a small niche and try that before she gave up. I asked her many questions and helped her put a plan together. She had 2 children in high school. I suggested that she go to the booster club president and talk to them about being able to market her products through the school booster club. At the present time they had someone that was supplying t-shirts and caps but that was all. The t-shirts had been screen printed. The booster club president told her to put a proposal together of what she had to offer.

She created some samples with the school logo on it and created a small flyer with pictures of the items. She was offering sweatshirts with 3 designs, placket shirts, and a fleece blanket to start with. They loved the quality of what she had and asked her if she would like to have a table at the school football games to see how it was received. She agreed to give the booster club 10% back of her revenue.

For the first game she made up a few samples to show the different options that she was offering and passed out flyers with pictures of her Spirit Wear! The parents loved the whole idea that they had a place where they could order items with the schools logo on it. She had a few orders that first time, nothing really great, but the parents started calling her from the flyers and waited for her at the games to place their orders. This grew and they wanted her to come to the other sports events.

Since she decided to focus on this one niche, School Spirit Wear, and place all of the marketing efforts into this one niche, her business started to grow from there.

From that she got calls for all types of embroidered products from these same people and her business really took off. When you focus on one niche, does it mean that you can only work within that niche? Absolutely not! It just means that if you focus your marketing dollars in one niche, it will save you a lot of money trying to market your business to the masses. You are still getting the word out about what you do. These same people that had children in school and purchased the spirit wear all needed gift items for every occasion and many needed corporate apparel for their businesses.

How Do I Develop A Niche Market?

Developing your own Niche Market takes a little time and a lot of thought. You may already have a specific area of the population that you are working with that you can expand on. You may already have a great deal of interest or knowledge about a particular subject that would help you to develop your niche.

You need to get away by yourself and really put some thought into your whole situation. The purpose of this is to get your creative juices flowing. When I want to get away and get into an environment that will really help me do this, I go to a park that is located on the

Susquehanna River here in my area of New York. I sit there at a picnic table overlooking the river and this helps me to relax. Sometimes I go to a coffee shop and sit at one of their tables by myself with a pen and paper in hand and block out all of the rest of the world.

I seem to be able to totally empty out my mind and come up with ideas there that I can't come up with at any other time. It is such a great feeling and I accomplish so much when I do this and always wonder why don't I do it more often?

Here are some questions that you can ask yourself to get this process stared!

- In what area do I have a great deal of expertise?
- What is my favorite subject?
- Am I crazy about Babies!
- Do I like horses, dogs, cats, specific sports, etc?
- What is my hobby?
- What type of organizations or clubs do I belong to?
- What do I enjoy the most?
- What types of interest do my friends & co-workers have?
- What types of people surround me on a daily basis?
- What do I have to offer that my competition does not?

Look for subjects that interest you and areas where you possess special knowledge. Maybe it has to do with former employment, or specialized skills. Maybe it has to do with tools that you have that other embroiderers don't have; such as the clamping systems or the cylindrical frame set. With tools like these, where you can get into areas of a garment and accomplish small tasks that other embroiderers aren't capable of doing with their tools.

Many times a new embroiderer will have a hobby or a subject of interest that they have been involved with previous to their decision to start an embroidery business and this can help to get them off the ground, so to speak.

Get out and mingle. Join a lunch networking group that introduce new business to the area. Talk to other people, see what it is that they want and cannot get. Go to trade shows of your interest or even shows in the mall, but always keep an open mind. Just like the Internet, where you start and where you end up can be completely different. You can have a very narrow niche that can broaden, such as Babies. Marketing to new parents can lead to marketing to grandparents. This can lead to everyone in the family, now your niche has broadened from Babies to Families.

Can I Have More Than One Niche Market?

Yes, you can. I had basically two different niche markets. One started with my children getting married and the other one was as a result of acquiring a son-in-law that was a police officer.

The first one stated when my son decided to get married and I was trying very hard to find something that was very personal and would be a keepsake. I wanted it to be a gift that no one else would give to the Bride and Groom. I decided to give them a pillow with their name and wedding date on it. Before I could create the pillow I needed a special design that no one else had access to. I came up with the one of a kind design, embroidered it with a freehand embroidery machine because it was a one-time item, and then made the pillow.

The pillow went over so well, that other people saw it and wanted one just like it. I then decided to have the design digitized and that was the beginning of a lot of gift pillows, wedding pillows, Mother's pillows, baby pillows and it even grew into police gift pillows. To make our pillows even more special, I always embroidered the name of the person that gave the gift on the back of the pillow. This was something that they would not be able to get somewhere else, at least not until someone else copied by idea.

I visited Bridal shops, department stores that had Bridal departments, and little boutiques to see what was available. I talked to shop owners and department managers to see if there were ever any requests for personalized items such as pillows. I showed them pictures of my pillows to see if they had any interest in them or knew of someone that I could talk to that would in fact have an interest in what I had. I found that there was a definite interest in them. I took my pillows to a catalog photographer and had some really good photos taken of them and created a brochure.

I put an ad in "Stitches" magazine to see if any other embroiderers would have an interest in them. I made the pillows with an envelope back so that they could easily embroider the names and sayings onto the finished pillow tops. This created enough business to continue running the ad for some time. I also had them displayed in my retail store and I took them to Bridal shows. I created a beautiful table skirt for my table with the same design that was on the pillows, on the front of the table skirt. Not only did I create a lot of attention for my pillows, I also created attention with other vendors displaying their products. They wanted a table skirt for their tables. But that is another subject and another whole market!

I sold pillows to Brides for their Mothers, I sold pillows to Mothers for the Brides and then this grew into christening pillows and pillows for teens. I still get calls from people that purchased my pillows wanting another pillow for a gift.

Second Niche Market Grew To Be My Largest Niche Market

My second Niche market all started with my Son-in-law who was and still is in law enforcement. He came in one day and said "Mom could you do this logo for me". It was his departments Police logo. He was in charge of a large region and they were having a special training on boat safety. He wanted the department police logo on some golf shirts for this training that he and some of the other troopers were going to be teaching. This was the beginning of a whole new niche market for me.

Each one of these other troopers that were teaching that course were from other regions and when they went back with their shirts, everyone was so impressed with the quality that we started receiving orders from those regions for all of their corporate apparel. We started taking orders for hats, t-shirts, golf shirts, sweaters and brief bags. From there, it just spread.

I made samples of many of the items that were requested and took them to a catalog photographer and made a brochure from the picture. I made up a price list and order form and sent it out to many of the surrounding area Public Safety offices. Officers from our area were moving into other areas and before long we were getting orders from most of the regions in the state. Next came the Attorney General's office and the State Senate and Assembly. It was great! Each time one of these officers went to a conference or any type of function, they took corporate items with them and traded them. Some of them traded patches, but the majority of them would trade hats or shirts.

We only sold these items to police officers and their loved ones. They had to show their police or department ID cards. We kept a small stock of corporate wear on hand for some of the local departments so they could come in and pick up an item off the shelf and walk out with it. I even came up with a small ID card and had them laminated to give to the guys for their wives, parents or girl friends so that they could come in and purchase gift items for their own police officer. They loved that.

Little Competition With Niche Markets

I did not have to worry about pricing or whether I was in line with the competition. They were not coming to me because of price. They were coming in to me because of my quality and service. Of course, it had to be a fair price, there is a limit to what someone will pay, regardless of the service or quality, but in general we had very little argument in the pricing arena. And therein lays the beauty of Niche Markets, prices and profits! As sales in our Niche Market increased, we actually let go of some our less profitable "other" accounts. Those sales required just as much work, but brought in less money.

Were there other embroiderers in our area? Yes, there were, several of them. Did they try and copy us? Yes, to a certain extent, but they could not service that niche the way that we did and were not willing to stock anything for them. I did not carry much of an inventory, but I could turn around an embroidered golf shirt or hat in a couple of hours. I always had on hand black, navy and gray golf shirts, t-shirts, sweatshirts and black & navy caps. I knew what they wanted because I took the time to talk to them. I had them tell me what they wanted and how they wanted it and then I went to work to give it to them. Actually to me it was a no brainer, it only made sense in more ways than one!

That is the secret of creating a profitable Niche Market! Find out what the Niche Market wants, how they want it and then give it to them. This is not hard to do. You must stay in touch with them, make changes as the market changes and be willing to work with them in whatever capacity that is necessary. You must develop your own little corner of the world in such a way that other people cannot penetrate it.

Okay, that is a brief look at what Niche Markets did for me. Now don't run out and start sewing Pillows and law enforcement logos because of my success! This may not be the market that would work for you or would interest you. Take the time to research and develop a niche that will work for you.

If you simply try to duplicate the efforts of others, you probably won't end up with the same results. Rather, you should use the experience and success of others to help you organize your thoughts and develop some potential ideas that will work for you.

There is a whole world of opportunity just waiting to be discovered.

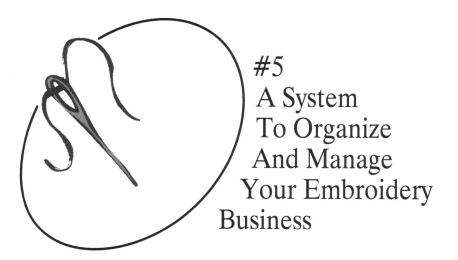

#5
A System
To Organize
And Manage
Your Embroidery
Business

In a balanced organization, working towards
a common objective, there is success.

~Arthur Help~

The Efficient Floor Plan And A Paper Workflow

One of the key elements to a highly profitable embroidery business is a good management system. Without a good organizational and management system in place it is very difficult to keep track of your business on a daily basis and grow your business over time. Before I start talking about organizing and managing the paper work flow of the business, I first want to talk about how to organize your shop layout or floor plan to get the best efficiency from your system.

Creating A Well-Organized Floor Plan

Creating a blueprint for a good floor plan for your embroidery work room is one of the first things that should be done to insure that you will have an efficient work flow. A layout for the most efficient work flow should be done in a loop if at all possible so that each area is not conflicting with another area. In a good work flow the work goes very efficiently from one area to the next. Without an efficient work flow, there are too many wasted steps from one job process to another. Below is a drawing of a basic layout for a small shop that has 2 embroidery machines. No work should be on the floor that is not in progress. This workflow is as follows:

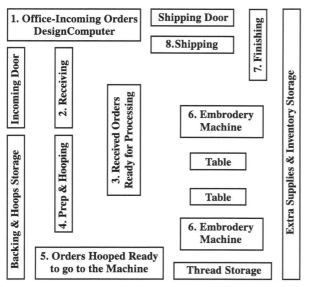

1. Order Processing
2. Receiving – Receiving should be located as close to the incoming door as possible.
3. Staging – Received orders waiting for the prep work and hooping.
4. Prep – where they are hooped and placed into baskets or bins ready to be transported to the embroidery machine.
5. Staging 2 – Hooped-Ready for the Embroidery Operator.
6. Embroidery Machine Production
7. Finishing – Garments are trimmed and packed. The packed garments are then ready for Shipping
8. Shipping or Pick up

117

If you are working from your home your floor plan may be a little different and you may have only one door into your embroidery room. If this is the case, Shipping can be located in the same area as the Receiving, but on the other side of the area.

The best physical layout of your shop will determine how you will be able to place your machines for the best possible production. The most efficient layout I have found has been having two machines across from each other with one wide table in the center or two narrow tables in the center, one for each machine. Another efficient way is a U shape having the third or smaller machine at the end of the U. One operator is assigned to each machine and a helper is assigned to all three. This helper can change threads, carry work, help load and unload machines. This helps the operators to concentrate on thread breaks and making sure the job is done correctly. In this manner more items are completed on each machine at the end of the day.

In the small single head shop or an in home shop, the Prep area and Finishing area can be on the same table directly across from your machine but keep your tools assigned in different locations at each end of the table and you will be able to function more efficiently. The Prep area should be at one end of the table and the Finishing area at the other end. If you have two machines, you can have both of them across from the table or one can be at one end of the table at the Prep area and the other machine across from the table. It will depend on how large your room is and how it is physically set up. Both layouts can be very efficient.

If you offer additional services such are sewing twill, sewing on patches or manufacturing banners, this area should be totally separate from the embroidery area. You may have more than one application on the same job that would encompass both embroidery and twill, but they still need to be set up in different locations. Different processes, machines and tools are used for sewing. If you manufacture banners, you will need to plan extra room for a large banner table. The banner table needs to be large enough to hold large banners but not so large so that you have wasted steps walking around it. My banner table is 4 feet wide and 10 feet long. I have used several different tables and this seems to be the best for most of my banners.

Create A Blueprint Of Your Embroidery Workroom Area

Before you start moving anything around, draw up a blueprint on a large piece of graph paper. Draw these pieces to scale and label them. Draw these pieces to scale so that it will work for you. Lay the labeled pieces on the graph paper and move each piece to the area that will represent where it should be moved.

Have every thread shelf, backing shelf or racks, hooper, steamer, etc (everything that you use that takes up floor space) in these drawings so that nothing is missed. Once you have your layout exactly the way that you want it, take a glue stick and glue them into place. This will help you make sure that everything does get placed in the proper location when you do make your move. It will help everyone that is involved with the move be more efficient. If electrical work or carpentry work is required, a copy of the blueprint can be made for the contractors. This will help to explain exactly what is needed and will make it easier for everyone concerned.

Organize Each Work Area For Maximum Efficiency

Each area or workstation has certain tools that are applicable only to the jobs or procedures that are done in that work area. Keep all of the tools needed for that area close at hand so that there is no time spent searching for the tools.

Each employee should be assigned his or her own set of tools. There should be enough for everyone with no borrowing between each other. When they have to borrow, they do not always get returned or get returned to the correct location. If each employee is assigned certain tools, make sure that they keep track of them. A good method is to have them wear an apron and have all of their tools in the apron pockets. This is a very efficient way of keeping track of the tools and having them at their fingertips at all times; saving a lot of wasted steps in looking for that needed tool.

When the employee is assigned tools, make a list of the tools that they were given, have them sign it and place it in their employee folder. This step will help to make them more responsible and they cannot deny that they were given a certain tool if it is missing. If they cannot keep track and keep loosing them, they should be responsible for the replacements. If they change position and they are assigned different tools, this should be noted in their employee folder. They should not be held responsible for tools that they no longer use and were exchanged or turned in to their superior.

(On my website you will find a Tool Assignment Sheet, www. EmbroideryBusinessSuccess.com/tool-assignment that you can use for the employee tool assignments.)

At the end of each work day the area should be swept clean and all of the tools, paperwork and unfinished items returned to the proper location ready for resuming the work the next day or for the person on the next shift. If the employee is in the middle of an unfinished job, notes should be created to let the next person know what was completed and what the next step is. All of the paperwork and notes pertaining to that job should be returned to the folder or on an "Unfinished" clipboard. If this is not done, it creates confusion and lost paperwork.

All of the supplies that are applicable to that work area and the function of that position should be stored in that work area. If extra supplies are kept on hand and interfere with the production, they should be stored in the Supply Storage area. This is especially true for a larger shop. You will store in the actual work area only the supplies that are needed in that work area for a short period of time.

The embroidery machines should have their own thread storage area behind the machine for easy retrieval or at least one central location that is close to all of the machines if it is not feasible for separate storage. The extra thread should be stored in the Supply Storage area.

The rolls of embroidery backing should always be stored in the Supply Storage area before it is cut into squares. After it is cut into the proper sized squares it is then moved to the hooping area that is applicable and the overflow should then be stored back into the Supply Storage area.

A well-organized floor plan is a critical factor when you are creating a highly efficient work flow.

Managing Your Paper Work Flow

Common questions that have been asked by my students when they are trying to organize their paperwork flow as they are starting or growing their embroidery business are:

- How do I manage my business?

- Where do I go to get the help that I need?

- How do I know what I will need?

- Where should I Start?

- Is there some type of software that I can purchase to help me?

So many people that start an embroidery business do so because they love what they do and are very creative. I was one of those people. They do not even think about the business side of the business. There are certain components that every business needs in order to run smoothly and create a profit.

One of the main components is a system for daily checks and balances to see if they are profitable. It is very important that you learn how to manage your entire business and it starts on a daily basis with each and every job. Whether you are a one person operation or a large apparel decorating shop, there are some important factors that must be present in whatever type of business management system you choose.

- The ability to create and deliver a quote very quickly

- A way to follow up on the quotes in a timely manner

- The ability to measure the progress of each order and it goes through each and every process.

- A way to measure your production

- A way to measure your profitability

- A system to keep track of your acquisition of goods

- A way to schedule your production

- The quick way to see if you can handle a rush order

- The ability to create a repeat order so there are no errors in ordering or production
- A system to see how quickly your money is coming in.

I have found so many businesses that do not have any type of system in place to help manage any part of their apparel decorating business. You can create your own management system or you can use one of the Business Management Software packages that are easily available for the apparel decorating industry. Either way, you must have one. This is a must in order to manage a growing business and become profitable at the same time.

Creating A System Without Software

If you do not have a business management software package, it is important that you create a system with spread sheets and a physical job board that will help you keep track of each step of your production.

- You must know all of your costs that are associated with each step of the order from Order taking to Invoicing.
- Create a job scheduling system with a spreadsheet that will help you keep track of each job in house and how long each job should take in production.
- You must create a job worksheet that will follow each step of the job. Each operator fills in the amount of time that it took for that step. At the end of the day, you must take these job production sheets and total them up to see if you were in fact profitable on that job.
- You can also use these worksheets to analyze each step of production to see if there is an easier and faster method for that step.
- If your production staff had any issues with the job, figure out why? Were the job orders incomplete?

- You must have a system in place to be able to give your customers an instant quote. This is very important for you in acquiring orders. If you cannot give an instant quote, you lose credibility and customers alike.

- You must have a system for tracking these quotes to make sure that they get attached to the customers work order.

- You must create an easy retrieval system in order to eliminate errors on repeat orders.

- Create a profitable price list. You must know how to price all of your products and services so that you are creating a profit on each job.

(To create your own Embroidery Pricing Structure quickly, go to HowToPriceEmbroidery.com This program teaches you step by step how to time each of your processes and create your own Pricing Structure. It has many formatted spreadsheets already prepared for you to help you keep track of your processes & create your profitable price list!)

Creating a system without a specific software management package is very doable and for a small one person operation this is a great way to get started. QuickBooks will work for you as you are getting your business started but if you have the financing available it is much easier to get started with a small software package that has been specifically designed for the apparel decorating industry from the beginning and let it grow with you. I will go over the basic Paperwork Flow system that you can create, with or without management software.

Paperwork Flow

When you are working with a customer either on the phone or in person it is easier if you have Sales Order packets made up ahead of time. This makes order processing go a little faster. I Just follow the system or the order of the packet. This makes the process simple and you do not forget the next step in the process. You will have all of your information in front of you at all times as you are going through the process.

Order Processing System

- Customer Quote Form – Can be part of packet or separate- Filled out and copy given to customer – your copy is stored in a 3 ring binder until customer comes back in.
- Order Form – I have one for Apparel and one for Caps – You can create others to fit your needs.
- Form of Payment – Credit card-Pay Pal-Check form
- Design Tracking & Timing Form
- Production Tracking & Timing Form
- Packing List
- Do you have a check list to make sure that all of the steps are taken?

There forms are all clipped together. When the order taking process is complete, you will make a copy of the Customers Order Form and the Customers Art work and start your process. The Original Order Form along with the Form of Payment and a copy of the Customers Art work is placed inside of a file folder that has been created for that Customer. You will then work with copies of the Order Form and the Customers Original Art work. This is your Work Order.

You are now ready to go through the Production Process. You will create a Job Folder. I have found that the Plastic Job Folders from the office supply store work great. Inside of the Job Folder you will have:

- Work Order
- Design Tracking & Timing Form
- Customers Artwork
- Production Tracking & Timing Form
- Packing List

• Checklist to make sure that all of the steps are taken. Each person will check off their step in the process on the check list when that process is completed.

Logging In System

As soon as the Order Processing completed you are ready to Log in the Order. You can Log the order in on the computer and then print out a copy daily and place it in a 3 ring binder. This binder will be stored on the Receiving desk. If you do not choose to Log in on the computer, you can create your Log in Form, print out the blank forms and fill them in as the orders come in. If you are a shop where you have someone that receives the orders specifically, you can have them fill in the form as they receive the orders and at the end of the day, it can be input into the computer. This is the process for many small to medium sized shops. The Log in form should include the following information:

• Date (the order came in)

• Job Number

• Customers Name

• Job Name

• Item Description

• Quantity of Pieces in Order

• Process (embroidery, screen printing, twill, heatpress)

• Date Due

• Date Goods Arrived from Distributor

• Date Shipped

The work order may come in from the customer by phone or email without the garments. The garments are shipped in separately from a distributor or manufacturer. Log the order in, assign it a job number and attach a copy of the order to a clip board marked "Waiting for Goods". When the Goods come in from the distributor or manufacturer, you pull out the Work Order and match it to the packing slip from the distributor. The order must match exactly.

- PO Number
- Quantity
- Item Number of the garments
- Color

You need to physically count all of the items and check to make sure that the color and sizes are correct and that there are no damaged goods. Notify the customer that the garments have been received and that there is a complete match or that there is a problem with the order and it is up to the customer to make whatever corrections there are to be made with the distributor or manufacturer.

After the job is logged in and counted it should be placed on the Staging shelving in the correct section of the staging area. This staging area should be divided up into sections for the type of work that is being done. The caps should be in one area, the small chest jobs in another area and the large jacket back or full front chest jobs should be in another area. Jobs that will have sewn twill applied to them should be in its own area. Each one of these types of jobs is handled or hooped differently. This makes visibility very easy for transporting to the specific prep area.

Order Preparation

After the order has been logged in successfully and before the Goods are received, the process for the design can begin. The design and sew out can be done and approved by the customer while you are waiting for the Goods to arrive. Many times the entire job can be ready for production as soon as the goods arrive from the distributor.

Send the Artwork to the Artist, Designer or Set up person to have it created. If it is going to be sent out to a digitizer, make sure that the artwork is ready for the digitizer to do his or her job. Check to see if the artwork is exactly what the customer wants, do any reworking of the design that needs to be done, and get the artwork approved by the customer before it is sent to the digitizer. This is very important. You will be wasting valuable time if you do not take this step.

When the design is ready to be sewn out, sew it out in the correct colors on the same type of fabric that the design is going to be sewn on. Examine the design to make sure it is OK. If not make your adjustments or send it back to the digitizer to make the adjustments and then sew it out again after the adjustments are made. Email a copy of the sew out to the customer for their approval or have the customer come into your shop, if it is a local order.

Have them sign off that the design is OK to be embroidered onto the garments. This is another very important step. If you neglect this step and the customer is not happy, you will be eating the order! Not a fun time!

You have a Design Timing & Tracking Form in your Order Packet. Make sure that you are keeping track of every step in your Design process. Each step is costing you money, be aware of it and keep track of it!

If you have to place an order for the Goods, then do so and make sure you have the right hoops, color of thread, backing and topping in stock. If not; place an order for any of the items that you are lacking. You want to be able to start the Production Process as soon as the Design is ready.

Production Process

Once the Design is ready to go and the Goods have arrived, it is now time to start the Production Process of this job. The Goods are pulled from the Staging area and matched up with the Work Order and the Design. It is time for the order to be hooped. You have a Production Timing & Tracking Form in your order packet, make sure that it is filled in as you go with all of the times. Do not miss this step! You need to find out what this order is costing!

As you are hooping the garments, you will place them into baskets or bins and take them to the Staging area where the garments are waiting to be embroidered. When the machine operator is ready for that order, or you are ready to embroider it, take the basket to the embroidery machine and start the embroidery process.

Once the job is embroidered, it will go to the Finishing area to be trimmed, have the backing and topping removed, steamed, folded, counted and placed into size stacks. It is then packed into boxes and the Packing Slip is filled in with the Quantity, Sizes and Colors. A copy is made of the Packing Slip and placed inside of the Customer's box. The Shipping Label is created and the Shipping costs are written on the Work Order and the box is taped up.

When a job has been shipped, go back to the Log In Form and fill in the date that it was shipped and draw a line through the entire order. This way at an instant glance you know that the order has been complete and has been shipped.

The Work Order, the Packing Slip original, the Artwork Tracking & Timing Form, the Production Tracking & Timing Form and the Checklist are all stapled together and sent to the office for billing. The Tracking & Timing Forms can then be removed to see exactly how much time the job took and you can quickly figure the cost and see if there was a profit made or if you need to make some adjustments in your process for the next order. This is another very important process. Many times we just do the same steps over and over without doing any evaluation and after keeping track of all of these steps and times we find that there is valuable time being wasted.

Choosing The Best System For Your Embroidery Business

There are several business management software packages available today but there are also many price ranges within these software packages. You need to know what is important to you and your business in order to be able to choose the right package. Each business is different and has different needs.

There are many software packages available that were designed for screen printing shops. Some of these will work OK for embroidery but you need to know for sure that it is going to work for you with your embroidery needs. I have found that some software company packages will work with any and all types of apparel decorating and some are decorating type specific. This will take a fair amount of investigating before you can decide which type is the best one for you.

You need to create a total snapshot of your entire business before thinking about which type of system or package you will need. Take an analysis of all of your business needs and answer all of the following questions.

- What type of software are you using for your accounting at the present time?
- How many employees to do you have?
- How many different types of decorating does your business offer?
- How many customers do you have?
- What type of business: wholesale, retail or contract?
- Do you offer products along with your services, or are you a service business only?
- What are your monthly sales and revenue?
- Do you have a concrete pricing system in place?
- Do you know what all of your actual costs are in your business that are associated with each different type of decorating that you offer? It is very important that they be separate in order to have true costing and pricing.
- Do you have a concrete way of planning for future growth?
- Do you have a way of measuring your growth and profitability?

Different Types Of Packages Available

Some of the Business management software packages have starter packages or entry level packages that will handle your quotes and invoicing. In my opinion; this is not enough to get you started.You must be able to provide your customer with a quick quote, but you also need to be able to take that quote, turn it into an instant work order and then into an invoice when the job is completed.

The advantage of using one of these packages is the ability to quote instantly, turn your quote into a work order, following the progress all of the way through and then turn it into an invoice for quick email delivery. You can keep track of your production from beginning to end and then you will know if you are profitable on the job after it is finished.

Almost all of the companies offer different modules that you can customize for your business and along with these separate modules they have different pricing options depending on your type of business and business needs. The price ranges for these packages are $700 to $10,000 to get started. It all depends on what level of business you have and how many different types of decorating you have in your business. For the small business just starting out, this is a bit pricey and QuickBooks along with my How To Price system will work great. I have found that QuickBooks is the most popular accounting software in the world. Most embroiderers that I know, use QuickBooks. It is a great software package that will work with most industry applications, but it is lacking in the management aspect for the apparel industry.

Many of the business management software packages will integrate with QuickBooks. If your business is a large shop with more than 10 employees, you may want to look at one of the packages that is a stand-alone package that will handle all of your accounting needs. If you are a small shop you may want to start with one of the less expensive packages that will integrate with QuickBooks to accommodate all of your needs. When you are looking for a business management software package, you want to make sure that they contain each component that is necessary for your particular business but each package should contain the following components.

- Reports that will tell you how profitable you are with each job.
- A job board that is available for everyone that is involved to see.
- An apparel acquisition system in place with integration to the apparel company that you use for ordering your goods.
- A system to create and deliver a quote quickly.
- A system to follow up with these quotes.
- A way to convert the quote to a work order and then to an invoice.

- A system to link the design with all of the details to the work order.

- A system to follow the progression of the order from inception to invoicing.

You want to be able to manage everything in your business with or without software, but having a software package makes it much easier to manage all aspects of your business. No matter what type of a system you adopt to use in your business, make sure that you have a system that will help you to create quotes in a hurry, measure the progress of each job, measure your production and measure your profitability. If you cannot measure it, you cannot manage it!

Here are some of the Business Management Software companies that are available. This is an incomplete list but these are the packages that I have researched.

Fast Manager www.FastManager.com
T-Quoter www.T-Quoter.com
Impress Software www.PreciseSoftware.com
Shop Works www.shopworx.com
How To Price Embroidery www.HowToPriceEmbroidery.com

#6
Finding
And Keeping
Good Dedicated
Employees

A business organization whose employees are happy is more productive, has a higher morale, and has a lower turnover.

~Mihaly Csikszentmihalyi~

Good Employees Are The Life Blood
Of Your Growing Embroidery Business

In today's world finding a good employee is not always an easy task. The questions foremost on any employers mind is where and how do I find them? Before you even begin to do this, you must take a long look at your employee compensation and benefits structure. If you do not have one, this needs to be in place before you hire your first employee.

- Are you willing to pay a good or competitive wage?

- What type of benefits are you willing to offer to attract the type of employee that you are looking for?

- Do you offer any vacation time with pay? If so, how many weeks?

- Do you have sick days off with pay? How many?

- Do you offer or provide health insurance? Is this deducted from their wages or do you provide it free of charge? How much is deducted? What type of plan do you offer?

- Are you willing to pay for their training or ongoing education or is this something that they will have to provide?

If you are not financially in a position to offer a high paying wage when this is a requirement for the position, then you must be ready to offer some extra benefits to compensate for this loss. This could be in the form of flexible working hours to fit their needs.

Where And How To Find A Good Employee

Word of mouth is the best way to find a new applicant but this does not always work out. Current employees may know of someone that is looking for a job. Tell your friends and family that you are looking for a good qualified employee.

Another avenue is the State Unemployment Service. Make sure that they send you only the type of people that you request. Many times they will send anyone that fills out an application and this is not what you want. Let them know exactly the type of person that you are looking for.

There are work programs that will help to pay part of your new employee's wages in exchange for their on the job training. Check with your local office in your state to see if they have this type of program. They have workers listed from companies that have down sized that would need to have training for a new position. These types of workers are usually good workers, very willing to work, do not expect high paying positions and are grateful for a new opportunity.

Place an ad on a bulletin board in a grocery store. Housewives or retirees are great prospects. They may not be able to work full-time but would work out great as a part-time employee and would usually give you their 100% while on the job. They usually have good organizational skills and work ethics. Housewives or home sewers usually have a lot of experience with bobbins and threading needles. Good dexterity is very important.

Call the local churches and talk to the minister. They may know of someone that would be looking for a position that they could recommend.

Go to the local college and see if you can place an ad. Many times you can find a student that will be a good worker and has a specific skill that you are looking for such as a graphics or accounting major.

What you are looking for in a new applicant it must be someone that is detail oriented, willing to listen and learn, can stand for long periods at a time (if that would be required for that position), be willing to work as a team player and must be willing to move at a fast pace when the pressure is on. When you are hiring someone to be a machine operator, keep in mind that this operator might be a good candidate for your first supervisor as you grow. As your business grows you need to have a continuous pool of good applicants to pull from.

The Interview – Asking The Right Questions

Before you start your interview process with each applicant you need to know the right questions to ask. A new applicant does not need to have experience in the embroidery field but there are basic skills that are required before they can even be considered.

- Do you have previous sewing experience? This is not necessary but it does help. They would already have basic knowledge of threads, needles, scissors, thread tensions and possibly machine maintenance.
- Do you have any computer knowledge? Not a requirement but it also is very helpful and shortens their learning curve if this will be a tool that they would be using.
- Do you know how to read, write, count and use a ruler? This is very important especially if it is a person that does not speak the same language on a daily basis. They will be required to read and write to fill in production reports.
- Can you stand for long periods at a time?
- What are your hobbies? Let them explain this to you.
- What do you consider your strengths? (What do you feel you are good at?)
- What do you feel are your weaknesses? (What do you feel you are not good at?)
- Would you be willing to tidy up at the end of the day?
- Would you be willing to clean and maintain the equipment that you will be using?
- Can you carry boxes full of garments?

- Would you be willing to move at a fast pace when the pressure is on?

- You must be willing to learn, listen and take orders. Does any of this bother you?

- Can you take constructive criticism?

- Do you have specific work hours that work better for you than others?

- Are you looking for Full-time work or Part-time work?

- Are you looking to advance in your position?

- Are you willing to be trained on a continuous basis?

These questions can be part of your application process on a questionnaire that they can fill out. After reviewing their answers and you feel that this is a person you would want to hire you can then schedule them for an interview. It will save you a lot of time in the hiring process. It is not necessary to keep bringing them in for a second or third interview. This is a waste of your time and their time.

If you have decided to hire this applicant, make it clear at the end of the interview, that this will be a 30 day trial and have a specific list of tasks or procedures that you expect them to master during those first 30 days..

Give them a clear job description and let them know that they will be evaluated on this description and specific list of tasks at the end of that 30 day trial.

How To Begin The Employee Training Process

The first day the new employee is on the job will be the most important day that he or she will have during their 30 day trial period. This period of orientation will lay the complete foundation and if done correctly will be the beginning of the training period for an excellent productive employee.

Start this day out by sitting down with them and welcoming them properly into your organization. Give them a copy of the job description that they were given at the end of their interview and again go over all of the points or the list of tasks that they will be expected to learn during their 30 day trial period. Let them know that this is exactly the same list that they will be evaluated upon at the end of that period. Give them a copy of the Employee Handbook and go over the main company policies to make sure that they understand them. Have them read the remainder of the manual and require that they sign off that they have read and understood it. (This is to be done on their own time and signing off can occur the next morning.)

If you have certain tools that they must use, assign them a complete set of tools. They are responsible for these tools for their total employment. Have them sign off on a form that they have received the tools.

(On my website you will find a Tool Assignment Sheet, www. EmbroideryBusinessSuccess.com/tool-assignment that you can use for the employee tool assignments.)

Let them know how they will be trained and who their trainer will be. The trainer in charge should be held accountable to you and the new employee should be held accountable to that trainer. Finally, give them a tour of the whole facility and introduce them to everyone.

A training program is a must for the success of any business. Each new employee must be trained thoroughly on one process before they are allowed to move onto the next process. This is true whether you are training someone to do the Order Entry, Shipping & Receiving, Hooping or as a Machine Operator. Each job is equally important and if one job is not being done properly, the next job or process will reflect it. This will result in a frustrating workplace. A well planned training program can produce excellent operators and create the right mood for the entire organization.

Basic Training Start For Production Employee

If you have hired a new employee to start on the production floor, the best place to start is at the end of the process, regardless of what you have hired them for. Start them trimming, folding and packing. This helps them to see how the process is finished and helps to get them excited to learn more. If a new employee cannot trim, they need to be dismissed. This is a very basic function, but takes a lot of dexterity and attention to detail. Many people feel that this part of the process is for low paying individuals that cannot do anything else. This could not be farther from the truth. A trimming mistake can ruin the entire process if close attention is not paid to detail. They need to have a positive attitude and their attitude will really show up during this process. I have created a program that will train these employees with these skills and will save you hours of time. You can send them to the website, give them the list of videos to watch for the process that you are training them for and then test them to make sure that they know what they are doing.

(www.TheEmbroideryTrainingResourceCenter.com
Over 175 training videos teaching all of the different processes)

They can then be moved into a helper's position. A helper is someone that can help tie new threads onto the machine, load and unload the machine, carry work from the hooping area to the machine and carry the finished work from the machine to the trimmers. The training of this helper is very important. They must be shown everything that they are supposed to do and thoroughly tested on these skills. This sounds like it is so simple that anyone should be able to do it, but they need to be taught exactly how each step is done.

Training A Helper

Step One – Show them where the threads are stored and how you put them onto the machine. Teach them how to do the Weavers knot so that the threads will go right through the needles. Make sure that they understand exactly what is meant each step of the process. Have them do it over and over until they have it mastered. Do not let them go to step two until step one is mastered.

(I have a video showing you an easy way to change a cone of thread so that the new thread will slip right through the eye of the needle so that you do not have to re-thread that needle. This is a huge timesaver!) www.embroiderybusinesssuccess.com/small-embroidery-shop-owner-train-employee/

Step Two – Teach them how to unload the embroidery machine making sure that they do not get anything caught in the needles as they are removing it from the machine. Teach them how to remove the hoop without touching the needles. This will dull the needles. Show them how to remove the hoop from the garment when they unload the machine and place both the unhooped garments and the hoops in their correct locations. Do not let them go to step three until step two is mastered.

Step Three – Teach them how to load the machine making sure that they do not get any of the garments caught under the presser foot or the throat plate. Teach them that they are not to touch the needles with the hoop as they are loading the machine. This will dull the needles. If this happens, the needles will be need be changed.

I have a short video showing how to place a garment into the machine so that the garment does not get caught under the presser foot or the throat plate.

www.embroiderybusinesssuccess.com/ step-training-employee-helpers-position/

These are basic skills but they need to be mastered by everyone that is on the production floor. This includes the trimmers, hoopers, packers, steamers, as well as the machine operators. This helps everyone to know what the whole process is and also gives you skilled workers to use if you need to pull them from another position to help out temporarily.

Make sure that the employee has a copy of the training manual that is applicable to their position and all of the processes that they will be expected to perform. They should be tested at the end of each training period to see if they have indeed mastered all of the skills that are required. It is too often taken for granted that the new person knows exactly what to do after they have been shown a couple of times. This is not the case as a general rule. Some people learn faster than others and just because a person has not learned as quickly as you or as quickly as you have expected them to, does not mean that they are not qualified to be a good worker. Sometimes a particular job position does not work out, but they can be trained for another position. If a person has mastered the skills of a helper but cannot go on from there, that is OK. They can remain a helper and be extremely valuable in that position. This helper makes it possible for the machine operator to get more production done by the day's end.

Make sure that your machine operators treat these new employees with the same respect that they want to be treated. This is not always the case. They very often expect too much too soon. Keep the lines of communication wide open between the new employee, the older employee, the supervisor and you. Everyone needs to be made to feel important in their position and you do not want any resentment, jealousy or dissent building up between anyone in the organization. Unfortunately, this is very common but must be avoided.

Training A Hooper

If a new employee has been hired to be a framer (hooper), they can then be trained into this position once they have completed the helper's position requirements. The steps of their training should be outlined in the Framing or Hooping Manual. This must cover all areas of hooping, as well as the proper use of backings, toppings and how the process is done. If you have videos available, it is much better to have them watch the videos first and then you can physically show them the process and have them do it. Quiz them on the types of backings and their proper uses before you let them try the process. Make sure that they understand what you are doing and why you are doing it. Test their tension in the hoop and make sure that the garment is hooped correctly and of course straight.

(www.TheEmbroideryTrainingResourceCenter.com Over 175 training videos teaching all of the different processes)

142 ❧

Training A Machine Operator

If your new employee is going to be a machine operator, then she or he must master all of the steps above before they can be moved into this position. An operator needs to know that the garments are hooped correctly and needs to know all of the problems that a hooper has in order to be able to check to see if the garment is hooped properly. If the machine operator embroiders a garment that was not hooped correctly, they should be held responsible. That should have been discovered and corrected before it was embroidered.

A machine operator should have constant supervision for the first two months. The first garment of every job should be run and checked to make sure that it is correct before proceeding on to finish the entire job. It does not matter how large or small the job is. This will prevent a lot of mistakes.

After the trainee has learned each machine they can then be left alone to run the machine without constant supervision. It is important to rotate the operators between all of the machines so that they will be able to run any one of them on a moment's notice in case someone else is absent. They should learn one machine thoroughly before they are rotated to the next machine.

Training A Trainer

A trainer must be someone that has completed all of the above tasks masterfully and has had at least three months of actual working alone on all of the machines. This person must be in the position to have the time to help a new employee without feeling that this is a burden. If they do feel that training is a burden, then they are not the right person for this task. This takes patience and understanding of that new employee. They must be able to answer all of their questions and they must encourage the new employee to ask any question that comes to their mind. It is much better to ask questions than to go ahead and do something wrong.

Teamwork And Expectations

Team work is not only encouraged, it is expected and if everyone does their part all along the training process, the new employees will be trained properly and this will in turn create a better atmosphere and working conditions for everyone concerned. If everyone does their part then there will be less mistakes and more production accomplished at the end of every working day.

The machine operators need to complete a Production Sheet at the end of every job. This will give you all of the information that you need to work with to make informed decisions about what is truly happening on the floor. A Spoilage Report should be completed if anything has been damaged and cannot be repaired. If a garment can be repaired; the time that it takes to repair it should be kept track of and the cost of the repair should be noted. The cost notation cannot be done by the operator; this must be done by you. The time taken to repair the garment is lost time from another job.

(At the website you will find the Production Sheet and a Spoilage Report to download and use.) www.embroiderybusinesssuccess.com/ production-forms/

How To Handle Needless Mistakes!

If a lot of mistakes are being made, you need to examine the processes and find out what the true cause is for the mistakes. Maybe it is the paperwork that they are using. Is all of the information on the paperwork noted correctly to do the job without any errors? If not, is the information quick to access? Who is the person that they should contact if they are missing a piece of this information? Maybe one of the processes is wrong or needs to be updated. There may be a problem with the supplies or the garments.

A thorough examination should be conducted before you attack any one person about the errors. The most important thing that you need to know is why they are occurring and then you can handle how to avoid another one. By tracking these losses on the Spoilage Report, you can find out if someone needs extra training in a particular area or if they are just being careless or complacent. This report is very valuable.

If you are having any type of employee problems, you need to identity what the problem is and make a decision as to how to solve it.

When people are trained properly there is less spoilage and down time and more co-operation. The only time the machine is making money is when it is actually running and it needs to be kept running as much as possible.

Maximizing The Efforts Of Your Employees – Benefit Options

Being creative with your benefits can be an affordable option to increasing wages. As a small business owner you cannot compete with the large employers for wages or benefits but you can create benefits that are not offered by the larger employers to maintain loyal satisfied workers in your workplace. You need total team work and co-operation from all of your employees at all times whether they are full-time or part-time employees. There are several ways to gain this loyalty and get their best possible effort and co-operation.

- Creating flexible working hours can give you employees that are excellent workers but cannot always conform to a strict work schedule of the 7 to 3:30 or 9 to 5 workplace. There are moms that need to be home until their children are off to school and must return home before the children arrive home from school. They also need time off when their children have that day off. This is very important to them, but at the same time, they would give you their best while they are in your place of business. Home sewers are a perfect example of this.

- You may have someone that is of retirement age and cannot work a fulltime schedule or perhaps one that need time off at certain points to care for a loved one, but while on the job they will give their utmost. They make good loyal employees.

- Treat each employee as if they are the most important person in the workplace. The trimmer or shipper that is often looked down upon is just as important as the highest paid machine operator. Their life, their wants and needs are just as real to them as those of your highest paid employee and they should be treated as such. Many times a higher paid employee will not treat these people in this manner and everyone needs to be shown just how important they are. This is one of those situations that often comes up in the workplace and it needs to be addressed immediately. This causes a lot of hard feelings, resentment and dissention on the floor.

• Make sure that you express the importance of each and every job position as part of the entire manufacturing process. The machine operators cannot do their job properly unless the hoopers are doing their job properly. Each and every job position in the business is dependent on the job position previous to it and after it. They all need to be done correctly in order for the next person to do his or her part correctly. This follows all the way thru from the Order Taker to the Shipper.

• Wearing a smile at all times shows your positive attitude. This is a huge reflection on the entire business. When you come out on the floor without a smile, the employees immediately wonder what is wrong. This is just the way it is. Make sure that you are showing your positive attitude at all times even when there is a problem present. You need to have the position that you are not attacking them for a problem, but you are trying to find the reason why the problem occurred in the first place.

• Maintaining a friendly family atmosphere in a small workplace is very important. One of the ways to accomplish this is by being present on the floor checking the work yourself. This does not have to be a constant action. This can take place occasionally during the day. You will gain more respect and they will try harder to please you. If they know that you personally are going to be picking up items and inspecting them, they will do whatever they can to make sure that they do their job correctly. Their main goal besides taking home a paycheck is to please you, their boss. It is very important to them to know that you are happy with their performance.

• If you plan to make any changes in the organization, systems or processes, make sure that you include them in these changes. Have a meeting to inform them of your plans and ask for their input. This will help to conquer their fear when they know that something is going to happen but they are not sure what it is. Production workers can be very insecure and will fight every change that is made whether it is a good one or a bad one, unless they know how it is going to affect them. This is especially evident when new paper work is being introduced. They feel that you are constantly checking on them and they do not want to feel that the boss is constantly breathing down their neck. They need to feel that they are part of the change and it will be much easier to get their co-operation.

• Have a group meeting once a week or twice a month and let everyone know how the company is doing. They like to feel that they are truly a part of the team and this is one way to gain their trust. If meetings are always held in private and they are not included, they become very suspicious and untrusting.

Wage increases should be given on merit and job performance alone and not on longevity. Using this method of increasing salaries gives them the motivation to keep striving for better performance and learning new job skills. Wage increases based on longevity alone does not motivate anyone to strive for higher performance. They have a tendency to become complacent knowing that they are going to get a raise based on the length of their employment and striving to do a better job is no longer important to them. This can cause a lot of dissention and hard feelings among workers that are constantly striving to do a better job. Yes, they do need cost of living increases but not an increase based on length of employment.

Surprise them and give them a treat every now and then. This is another huge way of gaining co-operation. It does not have to be expensive. You can give them a few hours off with pay when they have done something extraordinary. Make sure that they are rewarded for their extra efforts. A hot fudge sundae from McDonald's goes a long way in making them happy. This is something that I did about once per month and no one knew when it was happening. When I would come into the shop with hot fudge sundae's or a pizza, their eyes lit up and they were very happy! This has always been hugely successful tactic for me to gain co-operation and loyalty!

> *Executives owe it to the organization and to their*
> *fellow workers not to tolerate nonperforming*
> *individuals in important jobs.*
>
> ~Peter Drucker~

Employee Performance Review And Reprimands

Regularly scheduled Employee Performance Reviews are very important for a number of reasons. It allows you and the employee to have one on one contact with each other and this can create a feeling of trust.

The employee feels more confident when they know exactly how you feel about their performance. This gives them the opportunity to improve their skill level if this is what is needed. Sometimes they are not even aware that there is a problem and that change on their part is needed. This also gives the employee a chance to let the employer know how they feel and let them know if something is bothering them.

These reviews should be held at the beginning of every quarter. This will help to make improvements at a faster rate and problems do not get out of hand. If a problem does arise don't wait until the Performance Review time, handle it immediately. Too much time lapsing can make the problem worse.

Greet the employee with a smile when they come into your office for that review and make sure that you stay calm during the review no matter what the situation is.

The Review should be in a specific format with their job description and all of their duties and responsibilities listed. Discuss each one of their duties and let them know how you would grade their performance. A good method of rating that everyone understands is the 0-10 method, 10 being the best. Keep this in their record folder and compare it with their next review. This shows them that you care and have an interest in their personal success. They feel better knowing where they stand at all times.

If you do have to reprimand an employee, first find out exactly what they did. Have it documented and ask them how they think you should handle the problem. You may not agree with them, but this is OK. After you have concluded how the problem should be handled, let them know exactly how you intend to handle it and then give them encouragement. Do not hold any hard feelings or treat them any different than any of the other employees. Let them know that you have the confidence in them that they are going to improve or will be willing to make whatever change is necessary and that you know they are capable of achieving a much higher level of performance. Always end with a smile and you both will feel better. Make sure that you document what took place and file it in their employee folder.

Always ask the employee if there is something that you can do to help them improve their performance. Maybe a process or method really does not work for them or they are fighting a process that could be done easier. Many people are not capable of thinking through a problem or of finding a better way without help. If they need extra training to correct a process that is not being done properly, schedule the training and another review at the end of this training. It is to your benefit to help them in any way possible. They will become much more productive and thank you for it. They truly want to please you.

Important Records To Keep And Issues In Dismissal

There are certain records that are necessary to keep at all times on the employees. If for some reason you have to dismiss an employee you will need correct documentation to protect yourself against the authorities. If that employee files a complaint, it is up to you to prove that they are wrong. The authorities always take the side of the employee until you have proven otherwise.

- Application – Keep the application that they originally filled out when they applied for the position along with any questionnaire that was included. This will have all of their contact information on it in case you need to get in touch with them or notify someone if they have been hurt.

- A copy of all of the legal forms that are required in your state. Check with the state authorities to find out what these are in your state or county.

- Notes on the original interview and how you felt about their attitude and the way that they answered all of your questions.

- Any and all documentation on their Employee Performance Reviews.

- All documentation on any reprimands that they have been given.

- Any documentation on special privileges or benefits that you have given them.

- Their attendance record.

- All pay records including tax records of withholding, insurance and benefits.

- Accident reports. If they have been injured in any way, large or small this should be noted and kept in their file. If a report has been filed with the Workers Compensation Board, make sure that you keep all copies of any correspondence that has occurred between you, the employee and the Workers Compensation Board.

- Disability Forms if they have been filed. If the worker has been off for any type of disability all correspondence should be copied and kept in their folder. This includes any correspondence from their physician.
- A signed list of the tools that they are assigned when they are hired for their position.

Check with your local authorities to have the following questions answered:

- Do you have to issue any warnings or how many times are you required to issue these warnings before you can legally dismiss an employee?
- How many weeks of employment at your facility is required before an employee is eligible to collect unemployment compensation.
- If they are fired for a just cause are they eligible for unemployment compensation?
- Are you required to file any forms with the authorities if you do fire an employee? If so what form?
- If you have to lay them off for any reason, how long before they can collect unemployment compensation?
- Are you required to file any forms with the authorities if you do lay off an employee? If so what form?

Follow all of the rules to totally protect yourself in case you are ever audited or reported for any type of violation. If you do not have all of the correct documentation the authorities will give you time to come up with it, but it is very difficult to prove that you are right without having saved all of the required records from the first day of that employee's employment.

Learning to adjust to working with employees is not always easy, but if you want your business to grow, this is an area that you must master. You must learn to let go of the activities that you do and delegate them to someone else that can do them. This is another area that is not easy, especially if you are new to having employees. If you want your business to run properly when you are not around, then you will have to gradually turn some of the duties that you handle over to a qualified employee. I know from experience that this is not always easy, but it is necessary. When you have truly learned to delegate and trust someone else with your tasks, it is a very freeing feeling.

(Save yourself a lot of training time and frustration by sending your employees to the Embroidery video training site.)
www.TheEmbroideryTrainingResourceCenter.com

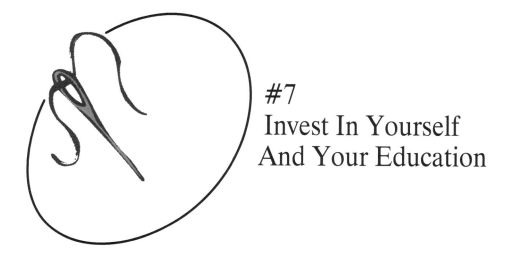

#7
Invest In Yourself
And Your Education

Perhaps the most valuable result of all education is the ability to make yourself do the thing you have to do, when it ought to be done, whether you like it or not; it is the first lesson that ought to be learned; and however early a man's training begins, it is probably the last lesson that he learns thoroughly.

Thomas H. Huxley (1825 - 1895)

English biologist

Continually Investing In Your Education Is One Of The Most Important Key Elements To Your Embroidery Business Success

Let's face it, starting a new embroidery business is hard work! It doesn't just take a little bit of time, it can take a lot of time. The truth is – most people that start an embroidery business simply do not have the skills needed to make their business profitable. Only 79% of the embroiderers that start their own business survive past the first year! Many more fail within the second and third year! This is a sad fact and it has little to do with the intention and effort of the embroiderer. It has more to do with having the right systems, approach and tools in place. They simply do not know the proven techniques that it takes to build a profitable embroidery business.

Trying to learn how to start or operate your embroidery business alone without the proper education or guidance is a huge mistake that many embroiderers make! Starting an embroidery business is not easy. Trying to learn all of the aspects of the embroidery business at once can be very overwhelming. Most people that decide to start an embroidery business have a high degree of intelligence, are very creative, have patience, and want to be their own bosses.

Investing in your education is one of most important areas of learning how to operate a successful embroidery business. There are several avenues that you can take to gain your education.

- Tradeshows Seminars – Marketing, Design Creation, Business Basics,
- Tradeshow Vendors – Many have a wealth of information
- Business seminars
- Adult Education Business courses – Management, Accounting, Marketing
- Embroidery Machine & Software Company Training
- Embroidery Training Videos
- Coach or Mentor

Education At Tradeshows

Going to tradeshows can be very beneficial. You will gain a lot of product knowledge from the Vendors and manufacturer's reps., or suppliers of the different products that you will want to market. I find many new and exciting products every time I attend the tradeshows. Product knowledge is very important in this business and a tradeshow is the best place to gain this knowledge. After attending a show, I am able to let my customers know of the new products that are available and this always helps to create new sales.

Every year the embroidery machines and software change or are updated. The equipment manufacturers are constantly upgrading and developing new time saving features to make your job go faster and easier. It is not necessary to attend every tradeshow every year but it is important to stay on top of the new technology that is available and about the only way that this is possible is to attend tradeshows.

Tradeshows also offer many practical training classes. You can get some business basics, design creation tips, information on the different supplies and even some marketing tips. Tradeshows are great places to network with other people that are in the embroidery business and many ideas are exchanged on how they are actually marketing or operating their business.

You need to attend at least one big tradeshow per year. You should not think of it as spending money, you need to think of it as an investment in your education. This is very important!

Business Seminars And Adult Education Business Courses

Many local colleges and business associations offer business seminars. I have taken many seminars that have been sponsored by the Chamber of Commerce, The Small Business Administration and the local community college. They are usually one day seminars and cover many topics on the business side of your business. As embroiderers we are very creative people and we love what we do, but we have a tendency to neglect the actual business side of our business. That is not the fun part to us, it is just a chore but it is the side of our business that will either make us or break us!

By attending these seminars I learned how to create a business plan, how to keep better track of my production and records, how to solve employee issues and even how to find suppliers for a lot of my business needs. I actually met my accountant through one of these seminars and it turned out to be a great relationship.

The Dale Carnegie Institute also offers courses in Public Speaking, Sales Training and Business Management. These are extremely valuable courses. They teach you how to work with all types of people and how to solve everyday issues within your business. These courses taught me how to actually manage many areas of my business and how to prevent small issues from developing into larger issues.

Embroidery Machine And Software Company Training

Most of the embroidery machine companies offer basic levels of training when you purchase their machine and software. They teach you the basics of how your machine works and how to get started using your software. They cannot go into too much detail because this is usually a classroom atmosphere with many people at different levels. Today much of the training is done on line and there is no interaction between you and the trainer. This can be very difficult. Some manufacturers send a trainer out to you but this is only the beginning of the training that you will need.

The cost of this basic training is usually packaged into the purchase price of your software so you really should take advantage of the training that they offer.

On-Line Embroidery Training

I have developed an embroidery video training site designed to help get you started with all of your embroidery training needs whether it is for applications, basic business needs or for training your employees. There are over 175 videos on this site that guide you through step by step many type of applications for running your embroidery business.

- How to hoop
- What backings to use for the different fabric types
- What needles to use for which fabrics
- Embroidery Design placement
- Machine maintenance
- How To Repair mistakes
- Applications training on Shirts, Caps, Visors, Jackets, Belts & Straps, Blankets, Handkerchiefs, Bags, Linens, Towels, Difficult Fabrics, Patches, and Appliques
- Business Forms
- Lots of Embroidery Tips
- And much more!

I also have another site that has a lot of articles and helps that will guide you along the way and help you on your journey. www.EmbroideryBusinessSuccess.com

Make sure to sign up for my FREE Ezine, **Embroidery Business Success Tips**, that I send out every other Thursday. www.theembroiderycoach.com/Newsletters/newsletter_signup.htm

Don't' miss out on your chance to receive a lot of FREE information with each issue.

Why Should I Invest In A Coach Or Mentor?

Starting your embroidery business with a Coach or Mentor, will shorten your learning curve and you will see a return on your investment much quicker! A mentor will help to eliminate being overwhelmed as you begin your business. I cannot emphasize this any stronger. I cannot emphasize this enough!

When you purchase your machine and software, you have 30 days before your first payment is due. This first 30 days should be spent working with a Coach or Mentor, so that at the end of the 30 days you have revenue coming in for that first payment, and do not have to dip into your own pocket to make that first payment. This is not the case is most situations. For many embroiderers it is several weeks, or even months, before they can generate enough income to make their machine payments.

A Coach or mentor can guide you step by step through all of the beginning stages of your business. A good coach will be able to:

- Help you create your Business Plan
- Help you with the right selection of machinery and software for your business.
- Teach you all of the basics of the business
- Guide you through the selection of tools
- Show you many shortcuts
- Help you with your pricing
- Guide you over the many hurdles as you are getting started
- Help you to create a web presence
- Guide you through marketing your business
- Save you many mistakes as you are learning your embroidery applications
- Show you where to purchase your products
- Help you with your selection of supplies

There are many opinions out there and many suppliers who try to sell you products that you really do not need. As a new embroiderer you just assume that they have more knowledge about what you need than you do. This too can be a very costly mistake. You can end up spending more money than necessary on unforeseen extra supplies.

I have to tell everyone that in the short three years that my husband and I have been in this crazy embroidery business, we never thought that we would get as far as we have so fast. Joyce's websites, webinars and personal guidance have been amazing! I can't say where we would be if it wasn't for her. Her vast outstanding knowledge of this business is just what every good embroider needs to become great! Thank you so very much!
Amanda & Howard Potter
A&P MasterImages
Utica, NY

My Own Costly Mistakes!

When I started my business and for many years after as my business grew, I made many costly mistakes! I then would have to spend a lot more money to learn how to fix those mistakes! This is not the way to go about learning the embroidery business. As I said in my Introduction, I am the type of person that had to learn everything the hard way! I definitely have learned and have spent many thousands of dollars on my education and still do today. Here are a few of the costly mistakes that I personally have made with my embroidery business!

Mistake # 1

I purchased a lower quality Embroidery Machine. Why did I do that? Simple, I investigated a lot of machines and saw one that was a lot cheaper than the rest of them and I thought, an embroidery machine is an embroidery machine. They all do the job so what difference could it possibly make? I found out in a real hurry! The machine that I really wanted was $10,000 more than the one that I purchased. One year later, and a lot of down time and costly repairs, I went back to the bank and borrowed the money for the machine that I should have purchased in the first place.

Your embroidery machine purchase is not an item that you should skimp on. This is an area, where you definitely get what you pay for. If you want excellent quality embroidery with little down time then you need to spend the extra money and purchase the right machine in the first place. The investment that you make in your embroidery machine should be one that is going to pay for itself in a very short time. It is your workhorse and if that workhorse is not working properly, you are not making any money. Time is money, and I definitely wasted a lot of both time and money making that mistake!

Mistake # 2

I made a lot of mistakes when it comes to software. The first time around I purchased one that was very inexpensive, because I did not know any better. It was one that was designed just for lettering. I was not able to do any editing with this software, so I had to purchase another package so that I could do the editing that I needed and add some stock designs. If I had asked more questions and was not just concerned with dollars at the time, I would have save myself a lot of frustration and money. I could have purchased one single package that would have done the job of both for a lot less money.

My next big software mistake was to purchase embroidery software that was a higher level than what I was capable of learning at the time. I was talked into purchasing the highest level of embroidery software that was available. The salesman told me that if I was going to be digitizing any designs, that I would need the highest level and that simply was not true. At the time I paid $34,000 for the software and computer in 1995. It had so much more than what I was going to use and I did not even have the time to learn half of what the software could do. I wasted many thousands of dollars on that purchase.

What I should have done was purchase a lower level of digitizing software and upgraded when I was ready. That would have saved me a lot of money. Purchasing the highest level of software when you are a new to digitizing really is not necessary unless you have the time to learn all about the software and how it is really going to benefit you to have the highest level.

I do not mean that you should not purchase high quality software; I just mean a lower level of high quality software is a better choice until you are ready for the next level. The highest level saves you time with some automatic features, but you must know what the basics are to begin with. The basics should be learned and thoroughly understood before you even think about any automatic features.

Mistake #3

I did not take advantage of the trade shows. I went to a few, but really did not apply myself and take the classes. The classes cost money and I figured that I really could not afford to take them. If I had, I would have been able to save a lot of time learning short cuts. I did not know what I was missing. Many of the classes that were available may have helped me to shorten my learning curve. The classes are taught my experts in their field and it is very important to take advantage of them whenever they are available in a location that is close to you.

Mistake #4

I offered low prices to get a lot of work. I knew what every other embroiderer was charging so I lowered my prices so that I would be able to get a lot more work! This definitely worked! I was working night and day; I was constantly hiring new people, training and also correctly their mistakes. This was one of the biggest mistakes that I ever made. It almost cost me my entire business! I knew what my costs were, and I was charging just over my costs but errors were constantly being made because of new operators. These errors ate up all of the tiny profit that I was making and it was costing me money to do the work. That was not too intelligent.

Sitting with my accountant and explaining to him what was going on was not a fun time. He made me realize that I would either have to rework my entire pricing structure and start making some changes or I would have to close my doors. Closing the doors was absolutely not an option, so I made all of the necessary changes.

Yes, I lost some customers, but that was OK. Many of my customers stuck with me and understood why I had to make the changes. When I raised my prices, I had less work, less stress and a higher profit.

These are just a few of the mistakes that I have made. If I had been working with someone that could have guided me when I was trying to make my business decisions, I could have avoided every one of the mistakes that I made.

Working Personally With A Coach

Working one on one with a Coach or Mentor will greatly increase your chances for your Embroidery Business Success. Yes, there is a cost to this one on one coaching, but it is worth it. Had I had that type of coaching when I started my embroidery business, I would have been up and running so much faster, with fewer costly mistakes!

It is so hard to make new embroiderers realize the importance of this education. When they first start investigating how to get started in an embroidery business, most of them go on line and research embroidery machine manufacturers, and see what they can get for information from them. The manufacturers tell them that you can get started very inexpensively, and of course they will train you.

The training that you receive from your machine manufacturers is very basic training. They touch on the basics and it is a general curriculum that they teach. They teach you more of what can be done with the machine and software rather than exactly how to do it. They go through the very basics of hooping, (maybe) and how to create a line or two of lettering but that is about it. Some will teach you all of the bells and whistles of the software, but they fail to actually teach you what you need to know to bring in that first dollar.

You will be wasting a lot of valuable time if you purchase your embroidery machine and software and then try to learn how to embroider, how to run a business, how to market your embroidery, and how to price your finished products without any guidance. This greatly increases the amount of time that it takes to start seeing a return on your investment. Each one of these areas alone has a long learning curve

A coach or mentor will plan out a training schedule and walk with you step by step to teach you what you need to know specifically for your business. There is no general curriculum when you are working one on one with your embroidery coach.

If you have already started your embroidery business and are experiencing any of the issues that I have spoken about in this book, maybe it is time for you to go back to the basics, get in touch with a Coach to help get you on the right track to profitability!

Working with a coach or mentor is an investment in your future. To this day, I still work with a Coach. I do not have an Embroidery Coach, but I have a Business Coach that helps me work with my business, plan out new strategies and helps to keep me focused. This has been an investment in my future that has been invaluable. Without my coach, I would not have been able to succeed as quickly as I have. Coaching from someone that is at a higher level in their business or education is very important. Without this I would get stagnant and stay at the same level of knowledge and earning power that I am today and to me, this is not acceptable. I want to move forward is my abilities and earning power each and every day.

"The Embroidery Experts Academy" is a program that I have set up to help move you forward on a personal level and help you reach a higher level in your embroidery business. The Embroidery Experts Academy was designed especially for those that wanted to excel in the business and become one of the top embroiderers in the embroidery industry. An individual program is designed for you and you alone. You can get help with:

- Planning
- Marketing Planning
- Setting Up your Business On Line
- Automatic Emailing System setup
- How to Write Email Follow messages that will bring in results
- How to Write Blog Posts & Articles
- Marketing Techniques
- Organization
- Day to Day Running your Business
- Pricing

- Working with & Training Employees
- Creating Training Manuals
- Newsletter Marketing
- Digitizing
- Design Basics
- Much More!

This program is designed for you so whatever you need help in to move you forward, that is exactly what you will learn! The more you know and put into practice, the sooner you are in the position of seeing the kind of results in your embroidery business that you can only dream of!

www.TheEmbroideryExpertsAcademy.com

Starting a new embroidery business in this economy can be a challenge, but if you do your homework and get the guidance that you need, you can make the journey to success a lot smoother and save yourself a lot of time and money.

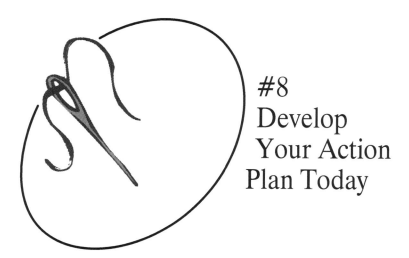

#8
Develop
Your Action
Plan Today

"You cannot change anything in your life with intention alone, which can become a watered-down, occasional hope that you'll get to tomorrow. Intention without action is useless.

~Caroline Myss~

Knowing is not enough; we must apply!

~Goethe~

Get Started On Your Journey To Creating
A Highly Profitable Embroidery Business

Now it is time to get started on your Action Plan. I have given you a lot of information in these chapters and it may be hard to know where to begin to actually create your own plan of action. Your first step is to go to the website www.embroiderybusinesssuccess.com/book-order-success/ and register your purchase. You will be able to download the Business Plan template that I have outlined in this book that will help you on your journey to creating your Embroidery Business Plan.

Creating your Embroidery Business Plan is extremely important and you need to get started on that process immediately. While you are working on your business plan, you also need to start marketing to your customers.

The easiest place to begin is to make your list of customers and start calling them. It is best to plan on calling a few customers at a time. Do not attempt to call everyone during the same sitting. Calling your customers personally should bring in more orders while you are creating the remainder of your plan. Don't forget your Thank you notes after speaking to your customers.

- Start tonight to create your plan for tomorrow.

- Make a list of the customers that you intend to call tomorrow. Create your scripts or download the scripts from the website that I have prepared to help get you started. It will make it easier if you have something to follow.

http://www. EmbroideryBusinessSuccess.com/scripts

- Schedule in some quiet time next weekend to get started on the process of creating your business plan. You may have to schedule some time each week or weekend to get through this plan if you have a heavy workload.

http://www.EmbroideryBusinessPlan.com

- Put some serious thought into your business and what you want it to do for you.
- Purchase a brightly colored notebook that is easy to spot and will not be misplaced.
- Divide your notebook into sections to match all of the sections in your business plan.
- Download your Embroidery Business Plan Template and add this to your binder. Place

each page section into the correct section of your binder. You may have to add pages, it all depends on the amount of information that you have.

- Start working on your immediate goals. Make sure that you write down your goals.
- If you do not know how to price your embroidery to create a profit, purchase the **"How To Create A Profitable Price List For Today's Marketplace."** This program will help you to run your business more efficiently.

http://www.HowToPriceEmbroidery.com

- If you have employees that need any type of training, go to the embroidery video training website and sign up for the membership program. You will be able to use your valuable time more efficiently while your employees are getting their training through video.

  http://www.TheEmbroideryTrainingResourceCenter.com

- Work through all of the areas of your Business plan that you can do yourself.
- Contact your accountant and show him or her what you have accomplished up to this point and ask for their opinion. Have them help you with the financial areas of your plan. You will learn a lot from your accountant and it will help you to be more knowledgeable about the business part of your embroidery business.
- Once your plan is completed, use this as your guide and refer to it at least once per month to keep you on track.
- Make any changes or adjustments that are needed at the end or the beginning of each month. If you have a specific time each month to do this, it will become a habit and you will look forward to it. You may want to schedule an appointment with your accountant to review the plan with you the first few times and then once every 6 months.
- If you are having any issues with any of the above action plans, get in touch with The Embroidery Coach. She will be able to help you get started creating your plan, guide you step by step and help you move closer to your goal at a faster pace.

Getting Help With Your Embroidery Business Plan

I created a program to help walk you through your Embroidery Business Plan step by step. It is a program that will make creating your Embroidery Business Plan very simple. I show you how to create your Marketing Plan for an entire year and I also teach you during this process how to plan out every department within your business. This is very important in order to have a business that will run efficiently! This is just as important to the small one person embroidery shop as it is to the large multi-head embroidery shop.

http://www.EmbroideryBusinessPlan.com

"The Embroidery Business Plan Course Really Helped Tie All The Loose Ends Together!"

I would like to thank you for all the great information you provide about running an embroidery business. It has been VERY helpful, particularly since I have decided to turn my operation into a full time business.

I have just purchased your Business Plan development course as I am getting ready to go to the bank for funding to expand the business. I have a business plan that is about complete, but I felt that it would be beneficial to get the input from your course, particularly on the financial projections. I do have spreadsheets from our local community college designed just for business plans to calculate all of the financial information, however, they are very generic. After reviewing Module 3, and the information you provided, I have to tell you that I am really excited now to wrap it up and get to the bank. It really helped tie all the loose ends together. THANK YOU!!!

Cindy Proctor
Busy Bee Embroidery
Dauphin, PA

"Your Website, Tips, Webinars, And Videos Actually Prevented Me From Throwing In The Towel!"

Your training is a God send. I have been learning things by trial and error. I should have joined your website 8 months ago. What you have on your website is invaluable to the embroidery entrepreneur. You don't know how instrumental you have been in moving our business forward. Your website, tips, webinars, and videos actually prevented me from "throwing in the towel." Thank you, thank you, thank you!!!

Jeanette B. Lee
Elite Embroidery
Columbus, OH

"It Is The Best Thing I Did For My Business!"

Joyce Jagger's webinars are a must if you are in the embroidery business. She offers classes on Embroidery Techniques, How to Price Embroidery, Marketing your business, Creating a website and much more! She shares her experience of 30 plus years with us and is always there to help.

Her website is filled with valuable information. I have had a Gold Club Membership and it has paid for itself over and over again, through tips and techniques, videos, webinars and more. It is the best thing I did for my business!

Monique Richardson
www.PersonalizedBlankiesandmore.com
a division of DESIGNS by Monique
Greenfield, MA

"She Has Given Me The Knowledge And Confidence In Myself To Run My Own Successful Embroidery Business!"

Joyce Jagger , The Embroidery Coach, is truly more than a coach. She is my Mentor. And why is that.... I started my Embroidery business six years ago, not knowing a thing about embroidery. Joyce has always taken the time to answer all of my questions along the way. If the answer is not on her Websites, or in her Webinars , it will be found with a personal one on one lesson. She has taught me everything about embroidery , designing, owning and running my own business. She has given me the knowledge and confidence in myself to run my own successful embroidery business

Tracy Trill
www.PersonalizedEmbroideryandGiftsbyTracy.com
Johnson City, NY

"The Embroidery Business Plan Course Really Helped Tie All The Loose Ends Together!"

I would like to thank you for all the great information you provide about running an embroidery business. It has been VERY helpful, particularly since I have decided to turn my operation into a full time business.

I have just purchased your Business Plan development course as I am getting ready to go to the bank for funding to expand the business. I have a business plan that is about complete, but I felt that it would be beneficial to get the input from your course, particularly on the financial projections. I do have spreadsheets from our local community college designed just for business plans to calculate all of the financial information, however, they are very generic. After reviewing Module 3, and the information you provided, I have to tell you that I am really excited now to wrap it up and get to the bank. It really helped tie all the loose ends together. THANK YOU!!!

Cindy Proctor
Busy Bee Embroidery
Dauphin, PA

The Embroidery Coach.com
By Joyce Jagger, The Embroidery Coach

"The Easiest and Fastest Way to Learn How to Start Your Embroidery Business, Learn Embroidery Techniques and Quick Embroidery Tips!"

Joyce Jagger, The Embroidery Coach, has developed many video-based embroidery training programs that will help you overcome many of the issues that you face when you are first starting your embroidery business. All embroiderers are faced with many obstacles on a daily basis, and it is not always easy to find resources to help you face those daily obstacles as you continue to grow in your embroidery business.

Joyce's video course, on-line training, one-on-one consulting, and interactive embroidery webinars provide new embroiderers with the skills to start their own embroidery business. They will:

- Help Shorten Your Learning Curve
- Help You Learn Right from the Comfort of Your Own Home or Office
- Save you Travel Time and Money
- Guide You Step-by-Step Through Each of the Embroidery Processes
- Teach You the Embroidery Application Basics
- Give You Confidence to Run Your Own Embroidery Business
- Teach You Basic Design Techniques
- Teach You How to Fix Embroidery Mistakes
- Teach You How to Work With Difficult Fabrics
- Teach You How to Market Your Business
- Teach You How to Price Your Products and Services to Make a Profit

The Embroidery Coach will help existing embroiderers improve their skills to provide higher quality embroidery and increase their profitability? She teaches you:

- How to Get the Most From Your Embroidery Software
- How to Get Your Business On-Line
- How to Set Your Business Apart from the Competition
- Advance Embroidery Design Techniques
- How to Find Good Employees
- How to Train New Employees

- How to Maintain Those Good Employees
- How to Increase Your Production Efficiency

To find out more about all of the products, programs and services she provides, go to TheEmbroideryCoach.com

Make sure to sign up for my FREE Ezine, **Embroidery Business Success Tips**, that is sent out every other Thursday. http:// www.theembroiderycoach.com/ Newsletters/newsletter_signup.htm

Don't miss out on your chance to receive a lot of FREE valuable information with each issue.

Made in the USA
Lexington, KY
24 February 2014